WITHDRAWN

EYEWITNESS
NATURAL DISASTERS

Hurricane-warning flags

Body casts, Pompeii

Fire truck

Buddhist statue survives tsunami

Planet Earth

Spirit of Smallpox carving

Doppler radar dome

Track buckled by giant wave

EYEWITNESS
NATURAL DISASTERS

Written by
CLAIRE WATTS

Consultant
TREVOR DAY

Seismograph

DK | Penguin Random House

REVISED EDITION

DK LONDON
Senior Editor Carron Brown **Designer** Chrissy Barnard
Senior US Editor Megan Douglass
Managing Editor Francesca Baines
Managing Art Editor Philip Letsu
Production Editor Kavita Varma
Senior Production Controller Jude Crozier
Senior Jackets Designer Surabhi Wadhwa-Gandhi
Jacket Design Development Manager Sophia MTT
Publisher Andrew Macintyre
Associate Publishing Director Liz Wheeler
Art Director Karen Self
Publishing Director Jonathan Metcalf

Consultant David Holmes

DK DELHI
Senior Editor Bharti Bedi
Senior Art Editor Vikas Chauhan
Art Editor Aparajita Sen
Picture Researcher Vishal Ghavri
Managing Editor Kingshuk Ghoshal
Managing Art Editor Govind Mittal
DTP Designers Pawan Kumar, Rakesh Kumar, Ashok Kumar
Jacket Designer Juhi Sheth

FIRST EDITION
Project Editors Jackie Fortey, Carey Scott
Designers Johnny Pau, Samantha Richiardi
Senior Editor Rob Houston
Senior Art Editors Owen Peyton-Jones, Philip Letsu
Production Editor Adam Stoneham
Publishing Managers Caroline Buckingham,
Andrew Macintyre, Laura Buller
Managing Editor Camilla Hallinan
Managing Art Editor Sophia M Tampakopoulos
Production Controllers Rebecca Short, Gordana Simakovic
Picture Researchers Celia Dearing, Julia Harris-Voss, and Jo Walton
DK Picture Library Rose Horridge
DTP Designer Andy Hilliard **Jacket Designer** Sarah Ponder

First Revised Edition
Consultant John Woodward

This Eyewitness ® Book has been conceived by
Dorling Kindersley Limited and Editions Gallimard

This American Edition, 2022
First American Edition, 2006
Published in the United States by DK Publishing
1745 Broadway, 20th Floor, New York, NY 10019

A catalog record for this book is available from the Library of Congress.

ISBN 978-0-7440-5638-9 (Paperback)
ISBN 978-0-7440-5639-6 (ALB)

DK books are available at special discounts when
purchased in bulk for sales promotions, premiums,
fund-raising, or educational use. For details, contact:
DK Publishing Special Markets,
1745 Broadway, 20th Floor, New York, NY 10019
SpecialSales@dk.com

Printed and bound in China

For the curious
www.dk.com

Deforestation

Mayan rain god

Hokusai's
Great Wave
painting

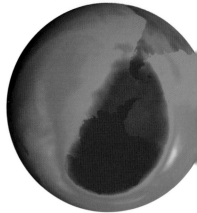

Ozone hole over
Antarctica

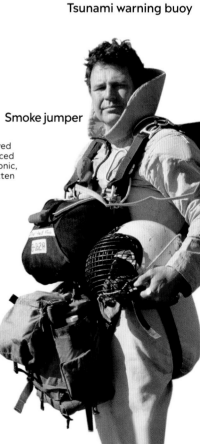

Tsunami warning buoy

Smoke jumper

Contents

Lava fountains erupt from Mount Etna

6
Dynamic planet

8
Restless Earth

10
The Earth shakes

12
Surviving an earthquake

14
What is a tsunami?

16
Wave power

18
Walls of water

20
Japan's terror

22
Recovery begins

24
Warnings

26
Volcanoes

28
Rivers of fire

30
Avalanches and landslides

32
Atmosphere

34
Wild weather

36
Hurricanes

38
Battling winds

40
Hurricane Katrina

42
Twisting tornadoes

44
Flood alert

46
Raging waters

48
Drought

50
Wildfire

52
Fighting fires

54
Climate change

56
Exploitation

58
Infectious diseases

60
Pandemic

62
The future

64
Did you know?

66
Timeline

69
Find out more

70
Glossary

72
Index

Dynamic
planet

Planet Earth provides us with the air, food, materials, and warmth that we need to thrive. But it also generates catastrophes, from tsunamis to tornadoes, that damage the environment and property, and take and disrupt lives. Such disasters may be sudden and violent, like an earthquake, or gradual, like a drought. There are more than 700 natural disasters every year, affecting about one person in 30.

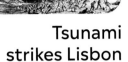

Tsunami strikes Lisbon

This picture of the 1755 earthquake and tsunami that destroyed Lisbon, Portugal, shows buildings leaning at impossible angles. Before instant media and photography, facts and images were often exaggerated.

Restless planet

Energy from the sun drives Earth's weather, and is the source of such disasters as droughts, floods, and hurricanes. Heat from within Earth causes rock movement beneath us, which can lead to earthquakes, volcanoes, and tsunamis.

Rivers of lava

Kilauea, Hawaii, is one of the most active volcanoes in the world, erupting almost constantly. There are more than 1,000 active volcanoes on land today that spew out fiery lava due to the high temperature and pressure deep underground.

Land heaved upward, leaving this house at a precarious angle

Devastating earthquakes

Earthquakes are one of the most feared natural disasters. This street in Ojiya City, northern Japan, was destroyed following a quake in October 2004. In the 20th century, quakes killed almost 1.5 million people. Survivors are often left with nothing, as buildings are destroyed, and transportation links, electricity, water supplies, and telephone lines are cut.

Blazing forests

Wildfires, such as this one that struck Big Sur, California, may be ignited by lightning or by a dropped match. They can destroy forests, leaving a scarred landscape, but forests have a natural ability to regenerate slowly. Sometimes, wind blows the fire toward an urban area, putting buildings and lives at risk from the flames and choking smoke.

New growth as first rainfall germinates seeds

A dry world

As the world's population grows, so does the demand for water. Human activities, such as cutting down forests, change local weather patterns, making droughts more likely. More than 100 million people suffer the effects of drought.

Deadly diseases

Most diseases that cause widespread illness and death are from microscopic organisms, such as the malaria-carrying parasite that lives in mosquito saliva. Malaria kills more than one million people every year, and 40 percent of the world's population live in high-risk malaria areas.

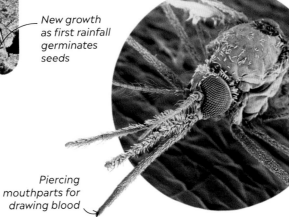

Piercing mouthparts for drawing blood

Residents carry their possessions as they flee the dangers of the erupting volcano

Escape

In 1984, scientists predicted the Mayon volcano's eruption in the Philippines, and so 73,000 people were evacuated. Modern technology, such as satellites that help produce weather forecasts, often makes it possible to predict disasters, giving people time to prepare and flee.

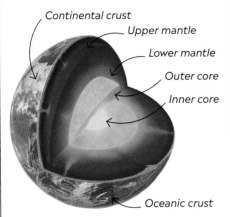

- Continental crust
- Upper mantle
- Lower mantle
- Outer core
- Inner core
- Oceanic crust

Earth's land surface is made of continental crust 45 miles (70 km) thick. The seabed lies on oceanic crust 5 miles (8 km) thick. The entire crust floats on hot, solid mantle. Earth's metal core reaches 10,800°F (6,000°C).

Tectonic plates

Earth's crust is divided into about 20 tectonic plates, which slowly move around Earth's surface, powered by its inner heat. Along the plates' edges, crust is constantly being destroyed or created. These processes cause most of Earth's earthquakes and volcanoes.

- Eurasian plate
- Arabian plate
- North American plate
- African plate
- South American plate
- Antarctic plate
- Great Rift Valley

Restless Earth

Deep inside Earth, the heat and pressures are so great they can turn carbon deposits into hard diamond. Earth's surface (crust) is divided into big slabs called tectonic plates. Some of these crunch together, others drift apart, and some grind past each other. The heat and pressure inside Earth disturb the tectonic plates. When this pressure is released at the planet's surface, it can cause earthquakes, volcanoes, and tsunamis.

Pangaea

Earth's tectonic plates formed 3.6 billion years ago. They constantly move and change shape, pushing continents together and apart. About 200 million years ago, at the time of the dinosaurs, all continents were part of one landmass—Pangaea.

South America and Africa fitted together

Earth today

Over the last 200 million years, the tectonic plates between Europe and the Americas have moved apart, opening up the Atlantic Ocean. Each year, the continents shift by nearly half an inch (at least 1 cm). The map will look different again in the future.

Atlantic Ocean now separates South America and Africa

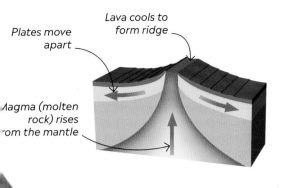

Plates move apart

Lava cools to form ridge

Magma (molten rock) rises from the mantle

Divergent boundary

When plates move apart, or diverge, magma (called lava once it reaches the surface) rises into the gap to form new crust. Iceland lies on the divergent boundary between the Eurasian plate and the North American plate. In oceans, most diverging plates form ocean ridges.

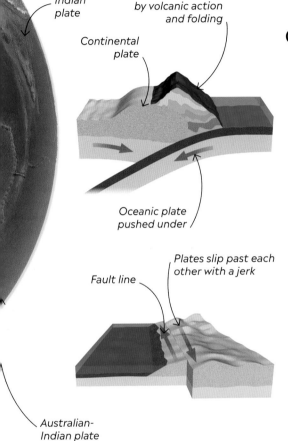

Indian plate

Mountains formed by volcanic action and folding

Continental plate

Oceanic plate pushed under

Australian-Indian plate

Convergent boundary

When an oceanic plate moves toward, or converges with, a continental plate, the oceanic plate is pushed beneath the continental plate, creating a trench in the ocean floor, and melting into magma. This rises through the continental crust to form a volcanic mountain range, such as the Andes in South America.

Fault line

Plates slip past each other with a jerk

Transform fault

Where two plates slide past each other, a transform fault occurs, such as the San Andreas Fault in the US. Friction between the rocks may make the plates jam. Pressure makes them jerk past each other, causing an earthquake or tsunami.

Steam rises as hot lava from Kilauea volcano in Hawaii flows into the sea

As lava cools, it hardens into rock

New crust

Wherever magma (molten rock) emerges from Earth's mantle, new crust is created. This may happen in a violent volcanic eruption or as the plates diverge. Magma also leaks through weak points in Earth's crust at hot spots far from the plate boundaries. As the plate moves over the hot spot, the magma may form a chain of volcanic islands, such as the Hawaiian islands.

The Earth shakes

Poseidon the Earth Shaker

In ancient Greece, people believed that earthquakes were caused by the god of the sea, Poseidon. When he was angry, Poseidon stamped on the ground or struck Earth with his three-pronged trident, setting off an earthquake. His unpredictable, violent behavior earned Poseidon the name Earth Shaker.

Earth's plates are always moving. Sometimes, they jolt, making the ground shake. Devised in 1935, Charles Richter's scale is usually used to measure earthquakes; the smallest measure up to 3.5 (enough to rattle a cup on a table), and the most severe measure over 8 (enough to destroy cities). Earthquakes cannot be prevented, but scientists can forecast some by studying past records and the buildup of stresses in rocks.

San Andreas Fault

The 750-mile- (1,207-km-) long San Andreas fault line in California splits the Pacific and North American plates, and generates earthquakes. Some parts slip regularly, producing slight tremors; others get jammed and shift as pressure is released, causing a major earthquake.

SEISMIC WAVES

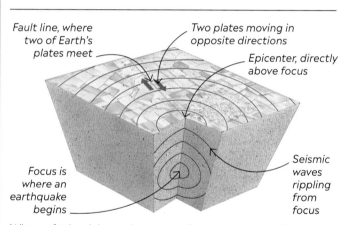

Fault line, where two of Earth's plates meet

Two plates moving in opposite directions

Epicenter, directly above focus

Focus is where an earthquake begins

Seismic waves rippling from focus

When a fault sticks, underground forces build up until rocks fracture at the "focus," from where seismic waves (vibrations) ripple out. The force is worst at the epicenter, above the focus on the surface. The most damaging quakes have a focus less than 40 miles (65 km) underground.

L.A. traffic jammed

An earthquake measuring 6.7 struck Los Angeles, CA, on January 17, 1994, causing this building to crush the cars below and damaging power supplies, roads, buildings, and a dam. People living along the San Andreas Fault are used to daily small tremors, but larger earthquakes are rare.

Haiti quake

An earthquake measuring 7 hit Haiti in the Caribbean on January 12, 2010. The island had no building construction standards; 250,000 houses and 30,000 commercial structures were destroyed, and 100,000 people died, crushed by collapsing buildings. Rescue efforts were hampered by communication failure and 54 aftershocks.

Earthquake detector

In 132 CE, Chinese astronomer Zhang Heng invented the first seismoscope for detecting ground movement. It shows the direction a tremor comes from within a range of about 40 miles (65 km).

Earth tremors cause one of the dragons to release a ball

Epicenter of earthquake

Colored bands are narrow around the epicenter, showing greater land displacement

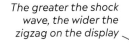

Ball falls into open mouth of the toad farthest from epicenter. The quake lies in the opposite direction from the toad.

Fault line

Ground movements

This satellite radar image shows land movement following a quake measuring 7.1 in California, in 1999. The colored bands show where people felt the same quake intensity, and where ground displacement occurred.

The greater the shock wave, the wider the zigzag on the display

Fine needle moves with tremors, recording the vibrations with ink

Revealing quakes

Earth tremors can be detected, recorded, and measured by a seismograph, which detects foreshocks produced by deep rocks fracturing before an earthquake. Monitoring foreshocks helps predict earthquakes.

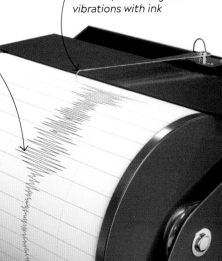

Surviving an
earthquake

Earthquakes have little impact in the wilderness, but can devastate built-up areas. In some earthquake zones, specially constructed buildings absorb vibrations without collapsing, but even they can fall down in a major earthquake. When an earthquake strikes, emergency plans are put into action: trained teams rescue the injured, fight fires, evacuate danger zones, make ruined buildings safe, and restore essential services.

Fighting fire
When the ground stops shaking, damage to electrical equipment and gas pipes can lead to an outbreak of fires. Firefighters have to struggle through ruined buildings and broken roads to reach the blaze. After the 1995 earthquake in Kobe, Japan, many of the ancient wooden buildings burned down when firefighters ran out of water.

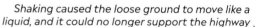
Shaking caused the loose ground to move like a liquid, and it could no longer support the highway

Trailokya Mohan Mandir at Kathmandu Durbar Square before 2015 earthquake

Trailokya Mohan Mandir at Kathmandu Durbar Square after 2015 earthquake

City in ruins
On April 25, 2015, an earthquake measuring 7.8 in magnitude shook the city of Kathmandu, Nepal, and its surrounding areas. It was followed by many aftershocks for many days. About 9,000 people died and around 23,000 were injured. More than 700,000 buildings and structures were destroyed in and around the city.

Searching for life

When an earthquake hits a city, people can be buried alive in collapsed buildings. Rescuers must find them before they suffocate, or die from their injuries or lack of water and food. Devices such as NASA's Finding Individuals for Disaster and Emergency Response (FINDER) can detect heartbeats of people and animals buried deep under debris.

Rescue workers need to wear protective gear, such as helmets.

The FINDER device is the size of a suitcase.

mergency shelter

month after Kobe's earthquake in 1995, 26,000 people were living in centers like this. he authorities were unable to accommodate who lost their homes; some had to sleep in nts or in their cars in freezing weather.

Highway buckled when waves rippled across ground surface

Shock in Japan

On January 17, 1995, an earthquake measuring 6.9 struck the city of Kobe, Japan. Road bridges collapsed as the bolts holding them together snapped. Much of Kobe is built on land that becomes unstable during an earthquake. The shock waves from the earthquake damaged 140,000 buildings and killed 5,500 people.

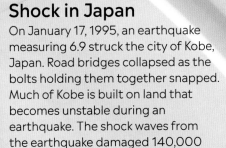

👁 EYEWITNESS

Rescue dogs
Trained dogs help rescuers by sniffing out survivors in the rubble. Frida, a rescue dog that was part of the Mexican navy's canine unit, located 12 people after several disasters, such as earthquakes, saving their lives. She is responsible for finding at least 41 dead bodies during her 10-year service from 2009–2019.

Special gear, such as shoes, worn for protection

What is a tsunami?

The first sign of a tsunami (soo-nah-mee) approaching the coast may be a sudden swell in the ocean. Tsunamis are caused by huge volumes of water shifting, usually due to undersea earthquakes. Traveling at speeds of up to 600 mph (950 kph), a tsunami can be a chain of waves hitting the shore at heights of 100 ft (30 m). Walls of water can slam against the coast for hours, stripping it of sand and vegetation, and sweep inland, flooding everything in their path.

The great wave

This Japanese painting by Katsushika Hokusai shows a towering wave. Tsunamis were called tidal waves, but now that we know they are not caused by tides, we call them by their Japanese name, which means harbor wave.

Soufrière Hills volcano in Montserrat, 1997

Clouds of smoke and ash cascading from Mount Pelée in Martinique

Volcanic eruption

When Mount Pelée, in Martinique, erupted on May 7, 1902, a torrent of volcanic gas, ash, and rock fragments, called a pyroclastic flow, fell into the sea. It caused a tsunami that destroyed the harbor.

Landslide

Tsunamis can be caused by landslides into the sea. As debris plunges into the water, the sudden shifting of water can generate a tsunami. However, tsunamis started by landslides usually affect only the local area and quickly subside.

Impact from space

Every day, hundreds of rocks fall from space. Most burn up in the atmosphere to become shooting stars. Those that reach Earth are called meteorites. If a huge object—such as an asteroid—hits the ocean, its impact may cause a tsunami.

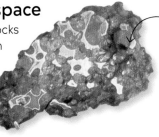

Meteorite composed of stone and iron

Earthquake

Most tsunamis are caused by earthquakes around Earth's tectonic plates. Huge crack in the ground can open up, as here in Gujarat, India. When this occurs under the ocean, tsunamis can occur.

Satellite image of a section of the coastline of Sumatra before the tsunami of December 26, 2004

After the tsunami

One of the worst natural disasters of the early 21st century began with an earthquake measuring 9 on the seafloor 150 miles (240 km) off the coast of Sumatra in the Indian Ocean. It killed more than 200,000, and stripped bare all low-lying areas, covering them with mud. Sand and rock were swept away from beaches; the sea was full of mud and debris.

The tsunami traveled
2,800 miles
(4,500 km) in
just seven hours.

Mud and debris
cover the beaches

Vegetation stripped away,
exposing rock and soil

FROM EARTHQUAKE TO TSUNAMI

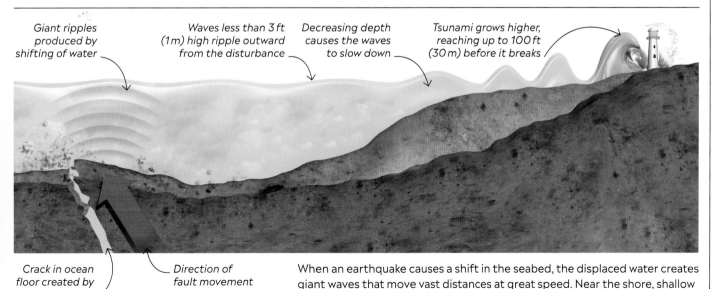

Giant ripples
produced by
shifting of water

Waves less than 3 ft
(1 m) high ripple outward
from the disturbance

Decreasing depth
causes the waves
to slow down

Tsunami grows higher,
reaching up to 100 ft
(30 m) before it breaks

Crack in ocean
floor created by
earthquake

Direction of
fault movement

When an earthquake causes a shift in the seabed, the displaced water creates giant waves that move vast distances at great speed. Near the shore, shallow depths make them slow down and grow higher until they break on land.

Harbor wave

On November 18, 1867, an earthquake measuring 7.5 created a tsunami that struck the steamship *La Plata* in St. Thomas's harbor in the Virgin Islands. Eyewitnesses described a wall of water 20 ft (6 m) high sweeping over the island's harbor.

Rock face stripped of vegetation by the tsunami is still bare 14 years later

Wave power

Tsunamis caused by earthquakes and volcanoes (tectonic tsunamis) can travel huge distances across oceans. Local tsunamis, caused by landslides, can cause higher waves, but do not travel as far. If both tectonic and local tsunamis occur, it can be devastating. The biggest tsunamis are caused by asteroid impacts. But it is not just the tsunami's origin that affects its power; the shape of the coastline also plays a role.

The biggest tsunami

On July 9, 1958, an earthquake measuring 8.3 saw 99 million tons (90 million metric tons) of rock crash into Lituya Bay, Alaska. A 1,700-ft- (525-m-) high splash stripped vegetation, leaving bare rock. A rockslide then created a 100-ft- (30-m-) high local tsunami—the largest in recent history.

Sea sculpture

The extraordinary towers and caves of Cathedral Rocks in New South Wales, Australia, were cut from the cliffs and gouged out in just a few minutes by a tsunami thousands of years ago. Scientists believe the rocks were sculpted by one of the most powerful types of tsunamis—one caused by an asteroid hitting the ocean or a landslide on the seabed.

Oil tanker hurled around by tsunami

Burning waters

On Good Friday, March 1964, an earthquake off the Alaska coast caused landslides that created a 30-ft (9-m) local tsunami in the town of Seward. Oil-storage tanks along the bay were damaged and ignited. Twenty minutes later, the first 40-ft (12-m) wave of a tectonic tsunami spread flaming oil into Seward, setting it on fire.

Wave or tsunami?

Ordinary wind-generated waves roll in to break on the shore about every 10 seconds. When a tsunami hits the shore, it rarely forms a breaker. There can be as much as 300 miles (500 km) between the crest of each wave, with more than an hour between the arrival of each wave. The waves generated by the 2011 Tohoku earthquake (left) reached heights of 33 ft (10 m).

Tsunamis and tidal bores

When a tsunami-generated wave reaches a river-mouth or a bay, the shape of the land funnels the wave into a narrow, high wall of seawater weighing billions of tons. Unusually, high tides create similar walls of water, called bores, as seen here on the Qiantang River in eastern China, where 30-ft (9-m) bores have moved at 25 mph (40 kph).

Walls of water

The earthquake that triggered the Indian Ocean tsunami of December 26, 2004, released energy equal to that of thousands of nuclear weapons. Ocean waves radiated out from its epicenter, close to the island of Sumatra, Indonesia; the strongest traveled east and west. Bangladesh, to the north, had few casualties; Somalia, far to the west, was harder hit. Some waves bent around land masses to hit the western coasts of Sri Lanka and India.

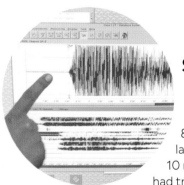

Seismogram
This seismograph reading shows the earthquake, measuring 9, that shook southern Asia just before 8 am, local time. Most earthquakes last a few seconds; this went on for 10 minutes. No one realized that it had triggered a tsunami.

Tide flooding Sri Lanka
This photograph, taken from a beachside resort hotel room in southwest Sri Lanka, shows when 33-ft- (10-m-) high waves rushed in like a very strong, fast tide two hours after the earthquake, and kept coming.

Before a tsunami, the sea can recede by as much as 1½ miles (2.5 km) on gently sloping shores.

The calm before the strike
Up to half an hour before the tsunami struck, the ocean appeared to drain from beaches. When the trough—a wave's low part—reaches shore, it sucks water offshore, called drawback. Many people went to investigate the exposed sand, with tragic results.

Banda Aceh

The place most devastated by the tsunami was the Indonesian city of Banda Aceh, on the island of Sumatra. The city was just 155 miles (250 km) from the earthquake's epicenter, and when the waves receded, it lay in ruins. One hundred thousand people may have lost their lives in the Banda province in just 15 minutes.

Buildings utterly flattened

TSUNAMI TRAVEL TIME

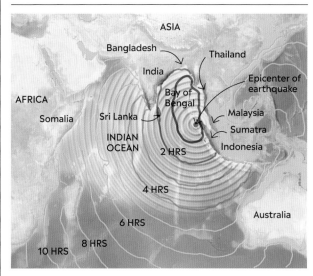

ASIA
Bangladesh
India
Thailand
AFRICA
Bay of Bengal
Epicenter of earthquake
Somalia
Sri Lanka
Malaysia
INDIAN OCEAN
Sumatra
2 HRS
Indonesia
4 HRS
6 HRS
Australia
8 HRS
10 HRS

Shock waves spread out from the epicenter like ripples from a stone dropped in water. Each line on the map indicates one hour of travel time. The waves took 15 minutes to reach the nearest land—Sumatra—seven hours to reach Somalia, and six hours to cause minor damage in northern Australia.

Wrecked boats, India

Livelihoods as well as lives were lost in the tsunami. All around the Indian Ocean, fishing boats lay battered beyond repair on the shore, like these in the south Indian state of Tamil Nadu. The tsunami destroyed two-thirds of its fishing fleet.

Twisted track

Near Seenigama, on the southwestern coast of Sri Lanka, 1,500 passengers perished when the tsunami hit the train in which they were traveling. The waves swept the engine and carriages from the track, and forced up the rails themselves, leaving a mass of twisted wood, metal, and tangled debris.

Japan's
terror

The tsunami that struck Japan on March 11, 2011, was one of the most catastrophic on record. Huge waves destroyed everything in their path. Thousands died as the debris-loaded water surged inland, flattening coastal cities, wrecking road and rail links, plus a nuclear power plant that released radiation and may take decades to clean up.

Earth shock
The biggest earthquake ever recorded in Japan shook the ocean floor 43 miles (70 km) off Honshu, the main Japanese island, and triggered the catastrophic tsunami. This building in Onagawa was destroyed by the earthquake and tsunami.

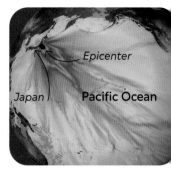

Japan   Epicenter   Pacific Ocean

Radiating waves
On the ocean floor off Japan, one part of Earth's crust is pushing beneath another. In March 2011, the boundary between the two gave way, raising the seabed by 23 ft (7 m), and creating huge waves that moved across the Pacific. The dark colors on this map show the highest waves; the red and orange, the smaller ones.

Waves reached record heights of **133 ft** (40.5 m).

Nuclear crisis

At the Fukushima nuclear power plant on the east coast of Japan, the nuclear reactors shut down automatically after the earthquake. When the tsunami hit 50 minutes later, it destroyed the emergency cooling pumps and caused the reactors to overheat. The radioactive fuel rods melted in three of the six reactors, creating pools of dangerous radioactive molten metal. Stored fuel rods in water tanks also overheated, threatening more radioactive leaks.

 EYEWITNESS

Cooling the nuclear reactor
Yasuo Sato joined the Tokyo Fire Department in 1975, and by 2010 he was the commander of nearly 1,800 units. In 2011, as the chief of the Tokyo Emergency Fire Response Team, he led a 138-member team that was able to cool down and protect Fukushima No.1 Nuclear Power Plant reactor from further meltdown and radiation leaks.

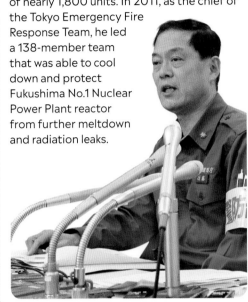

Surging water

When the tsunami reached shallow water, its waves slowed down and rose far higher than thought possible, overwhelming the tsunami-resistant sea defenses, as seen here at the fishing port of Miyako. Here, the sea rose to at least 28 ft (8.5 m) above normal high-tide level, lifting cars over the sea wall and ripping boats from their moorings.

Debris piled up by the tsunami waves

Innocent victims

The earthquake and tsunami killed more than 18,000 people—90 percent of them drowned by the raging floodwaters. Many more were left homeless, including at least 100,000 children. Here, a shocked survivor gazes at the destruction in Ishinomaki, where one school lost 74 of its 108 students.

Desperate rescue

When the giant waves finally stopped, survivors and rescue workers combed through the wreckage for trapped victims. This young girl was rescued from Kesennuma, a fishing port north of the earthquake's epicenter that suffered the earthquake, tsunami, and fires.

Recovery
begins

In memory
This Buddhist statue was left on the beach at Khao Lak, Thailand, in memory of those killed in the 2004 Asian tsunami. Religious services were held all along the coast.

Following a tsunami disaster, aid comes from around the globe. The first task is to provide shelter and medical care. Then, the debris left by the water must be cleared, and so must victims' bodies before they start to rot and spread disease. Once the clearing is done, people can get back to normal life. But recovery can be slow, with vital infrastructure destroyed and people suffering from shock and grief.

Health check
A child is checked for radiatio exposure in Fukushima, Japar after the 2011 tsunami damaged Fukushima's nuclea reactors, and dangerous amounts of radiation leaked out. Local people were evacuated, but will need health checks for many years to come.

Refugee camp at Bang Muang, Phang Tha, in Thailand

Tent city
Vast camps housed people who were made homeless by the 2004 Asian tsunami. Poor sanitation in huge refugee camps can lead to outbreaks of diseases such as cholera and typhoid. This was prevented by health services, which provided safe drinking water and food, the means to cook, and adequate sanitation.

Elephants at work
After the 2004 Asian tsunami, corpses had to be buried quickly to prevent outbreaks of disease. Thailand's elephants were able to reach otherwise inaccessible areas. First, dogs sniffed out bodies, then the elephants nudged aside building ruins or fallen trees to reveal the corpses beneath. They also moved the bodies to burial sites.

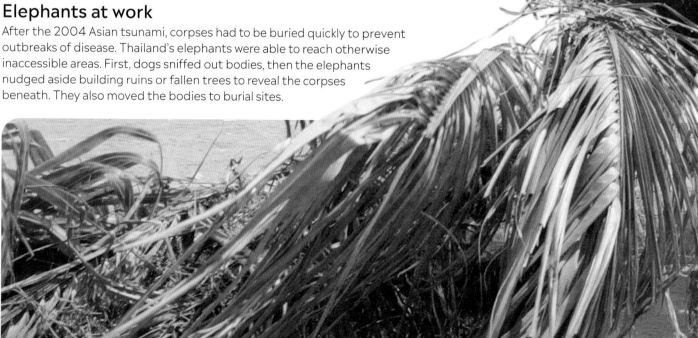

Clearing the damage

Rescuers search for missing residents in Miyagi prefecture, four days after the March 11, 2011, earthquake and tsunami. Japan's government asked people not to panic-buy food and supplies in the aftermath.

Elephant handler wears mask as protection against the smell of decaying bodies

Boat building

On coasts hit by the 2004 Asian tsunami, local people had to rebuild boats that had been damaged by the waves. Boats are vital to the region's fishing industry, but many tourist resorts also use them to show visitors the coral reefs.

Boat building on the beach at Phuket, Thailand

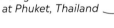

Back to school

These children at an elementary school in Natori, northern Japan, lost many of their friends when the school was flooded during the 2011 Japanese tsunami. Many were also made homeless when their houses were swept away.

Warnings

In 2004, the Asian tsunami struck the Indian Ocean out of the blue. In the Pacific, there was a tsunami warning system. Oceanographers monitored the ocean for possible tsunamis, and used sirens and broadcasts to warn people. In 2006, a similar program was set up in the Indian Ocean, but all such systems are limited. The earthquake that triggered the 2011 tsunami was so close to Japan that people on the coast had little time to escape.

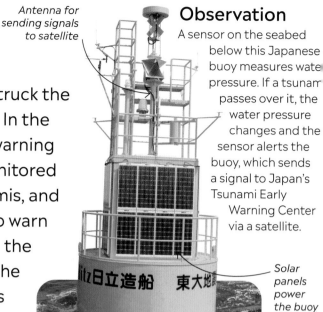

Antenna for sending signals to satellite

Observation

A sensor on the seabed below this Japanese buoy measures water pressure. If a tsunami passes over it, the water pressure changes and the sensor alerts the buoy, which sends a signal to Japan's Tsunami Early Warning Center via a satellite.

Solar panels power the buoy

Holding back the wave

This enormous floodgate in Namazu Port, Japan, has door 30 ft (9.3 m) high, which automatically shuts if seismograph senses an earthquake that could lead to tsunami. Most of Japan's population lives along th coast, so measures like this offer vita protection to the region earthquake-prone citie

Gate raised to allow tall ships into the harbor

Massive gate weighs 925 tons (840 metric tons)

ntil the end

uring the 2011 tsunami, Miki Endo, worker at the Crisis Management epartment, in Minamisanriku, pan, continued to issue warnings er a loudspeaker system until e center was overcome by sea. day, people visit the ruined ell of the center to pay spect and remember those o died, including Miki.

Tsunami Warning Tower

Tsunami warning centers gather data continuously and predict where and when a tsunami will arrive. Warning towers, like this one in Thailand, are built around the Indian Ocean. They have sirens, and antennae that can interrupt TV and radio broadcasts to send text messages that advise people to move to higher ground, away from the coast.

Two radar altimeters measure sea surface height

he sea from space

unched in 1992, the Poseidon satellite records a surface height and ocean currents from its bit above Earth. Tiny changes in sea level after undersea earthquake can give advance arning of a tsunami.

Sonar device

The first step for a tsunami warning system is to monitor earthquake activity on the seabed. This sonar device mapped the Indian Ocean seabed near Banda Aceh, where the 2004 tsunami originated. It reflects sound off the seabed to build a 3D image.

THE OCEAN FLOOR IN 3D

Land areas above sea level

Areas below sea level are blue/green

Steep slope leading to ocean depths

Sonar maps, like this 3D image of the seabed around California, enable oceanographers to study the ocean-floor's contours. Regular scanning shows seabed movement, such as shifts along a fault line, which could signal tsunami-triggering events.

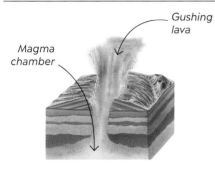

Magma chamber

Gushing lava

Shield cone volcano

Runny lava erupts from the vent in a gushing river, or fountain. This runny lava spreads over a wide area. Later eruptions form a mountain with gently sloping sides. A typical shield cone volcano is Mauna Kea in Hawaii.

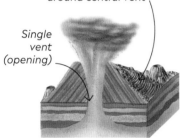

Cone formed by ash and rocks piling steeply around central vent

Single vent (opening)

Cinder cone volcano

These volcanoes usually have one vent that erupts ash and rocks that fall in a ring. The straight-sided cone is formed from erupted rocks. Cinder cones, such as Paricutin in Mexico, are rarely over 1,000 ft (300 m) above land.

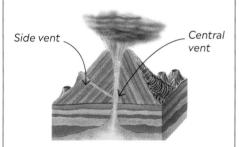

Side vent

Central vent

Stratovolcano

Thick, sticky lava cools and hardens quickly to produce a steep mountain. Rocky, ashy eruptions alternate with lava, creating layers in the cone- or dome-shaped mountain, which may grow 10,000 ft (3,050 m) high.

Volcanoes

Pockets of hot molten (liquid) rock called magma lie underneath Earth's solid crust. Magma rises to the surface through weak spots in the crust—most of which lie on the margins of Earth's tectonic plates. As magma pushes up, pressure builds until magma breaks through Earth's crust, sending rock, ash, and lava crashing onto the surface as a volcano.

Goddess Pele

Legend says that the Hawaiian goddess of volcanoes, Pele, has a volcano's powers to melt rocks, destroy forests, make mountains, and build new islands.

Molten lava sets fire to trees

Cracks and ridges form as the lava sheet hardens

Birth of an island

Most volcanic eruptions occur under the oceans. In 1963, an eruption near Iceland made the sea steam, as seawater poured into the volcano's vent and was boiled by its heat. Over a few years, volcanic lava and ash piled up into a small island—Surtsey.

Ashy steam blasting from the volcano's vent

Sleeping volcano

Japan's Mount Fuji last erupted in 1707 and is now dormant—it shows no sign of activity, but may erupt in the future. Active volcanoes frequently erupt. Volcanoes that have been dormant for thousands of years are called extinct—but they may erupt again.

Fiery river

When magma inside a volcano is runny and does not contain much gas, it erupts in a hot stream of lava, like this in Hawaii. When the magma is thick and sticky, it traps gases, such as steam and carbon dioxide, inside it. Sticky, viscous magma erupts in a violent explosion of lava globules and burning ash.

Temperature taking

Volcanologists (volcano scientists) measure the ground temperature around volcanic vents to find out what is going on beneath Earth's surface. Active volcanoes are monitored frequently, so that people can be warned if the ground temperature rises and an eruption is likely.

Taking samples

After eruptions, volcanologists in heat-protective suits collect fresh lava samples. These samples can show changes in a volcano's behavior. For example, different gas mixtures may make it more explosive.

Plume of volcanic ash

Rivers of fire

An exploding volcano is a magnificent sight, as enormous pressures force lava, ash, rocks, and superheated gases out of Earth. After an eruption, soil may be nourished with mineral-rich volcanic ash which is good for farming. Today, eruptions can be predicted and people can be evacuated from the danger zone. However, a major eruption can affect weather around the world.

Mount St. Helens

When Mount St. Helens in Washington erupted on May 18, 1980, so much rock was blown off its top that it lost 1,312 ft (400 m) in height. A cloud of ash spread over 20,000 sq miles (50,000 sq km), causing a major hazard for aircraft. In 2010, a similar ash cloud was spewed out by the Eyjafjallajökull volcano in Iceland.

👁 EYEWITNESS

Studying an eruption
American David Johnston (1949–1980) was one of the first volcanologists to arrive at Mount St. Helens a day before it began erupting in 1980. Johnston convinced the authorities to restrict access to the area around the volcano, which saved many lives when it finally erupted. Tragically, he was killed by the eruption.

Moss   *Lichen*   *Fern*

New life

The first plants to appear in solidified lava after an eruption are mosses, lichens, and ferns. Volcanic rock may take decades to become fertile soil for larger plants to take root.

Pyroclastic flow

On June 15, 1991, Mount Pinatubo in the Philippines, began erupting after lying dormant for 600 years. Rock particles and ash flew 25 miles (40 km) into the atmosphere. This deadly cloud of hot gas and debris, called a pyroclastic flow, hurtled at speeds of 100 mph (160 kph) across the surrounding area.

Deadly dust

As ash from Mount Pinatubo filled the air with a choking cloud and covered the fields, farmers took buffalo to look for unaffected areas. Many developed pneumonia from inhaling the gritty ash, and entire harvests were lost.

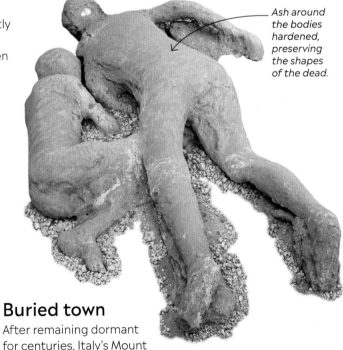

Jets of fire

In 2001, Italy's 11,120-ft- (3,390-m-) high Mount Etna exploded with a bang. Etna is one of Europe's highest mountains and its most active volcano. Usually, it erupts in small, continuous bursts. Lava flows constantly damage roads and property, and threaten towns. Concrete barriers, trenches, even explosives, have been used to try to redirect the lava, with limited success.

Ash around the bodies hardened, preserving the shapes of the dead.

Frequent eruptions

One of the highest volcanoes in Java, Indonesia, Mount Semeru is also one of the most active. In December 2021, it experienced one of its largest eruptions in recent history, producing an avalanche of hot cloud and heavy ashfall.

Buried town

After remaining dormant for centuries, Italy's Mount Vesuvius erupted on August 24, 79 CE. Some 2,000 people died of suffocation in the town of Pompeii, which lay in the shadow of the volcano. The dead were buried under 100 ft (30 m) of ash; no remains were discovered until excavations began in 1860.

Avalanches and **landslides**

When gravity's pull is greater than the forces that hold rock and snow together on a steep hillside, the rock and snow may crash down the slope. Unstable rocks and soil can cause a landslide, while snow can hurtle as an avalanche, burying anything in its path. Speedy rescue is essential to save buried survivors; for hundreds of years, rescue dogs have helped find trapped people.

St. Berna[r]
rescue do[g]

To the rescue

High in the mountains, rescue teams use helicopters to reach injured people quickly. A winch is used to lower rescuers and haul up the injured on stretchers. The pilot must be careful because even the noise and draft of a helicopter can trigger another avalanche.

Avalanche warning sign

In mountain ski resorts, warnin[g] signs indicate avalanche risk. It is difficult to predict exactly when and where an avalanche will occur, but experts can tell when the snow layers become unstable enough to trigger an avalanche.

Torrent of snow

When mountain snow builds into an unstable overhang, or thaws and becomes loose, an earth tremor or loud noise can cause an avalanche. As it rushes down the slope, the avalanche loosens more snow and picks up rocks and soil. It can be ½ mile (800 m) wide. Anyone caught in it has a five percent chance of survival.

Avalanche preventio[n]

Fences built across slopes can sto[p] tumbling snow before it grows into [a] huge avalanche. Sometimes, explosive[s] are used to trigger small avalanches. Th[is] prevents the buildup of too much sno[w] that could cause a major avalanche[.]

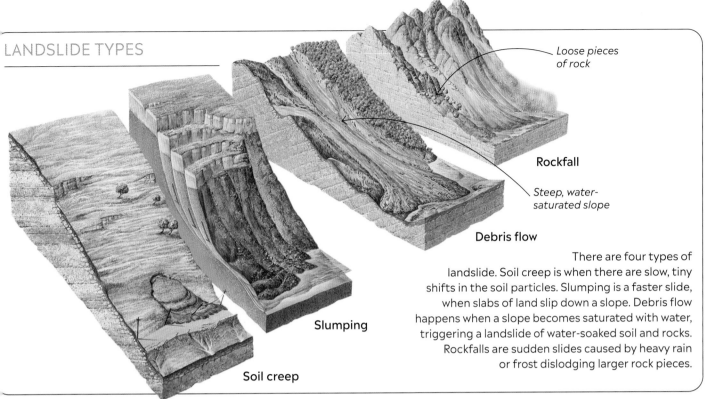

Loose pieces of rock

Rockfall

Steep, water-saturated slope

Debris flow

There are four types of landslide. Soil creep is when there are slow, tiny shifts in the soil particles. Slumping is a faster slide, when slabs of land slip down a slope. Debris flow happens when a slope becomes saturated with water, triggering a landslide of water-soaked soil and rocks. Rockfalls are sudden slides caused by heavy rain or frost dislodging larger rock pieces.

Slumping

Soil creep

Rocky road

In August 1983, a 20-ft (6-m) slab of granite crashed from the hillside onto the highway in Yosemite National Park in California. Rockfalls along roads are often the result of poor road-building methods.

Rescuers carry the body of a landslide victim

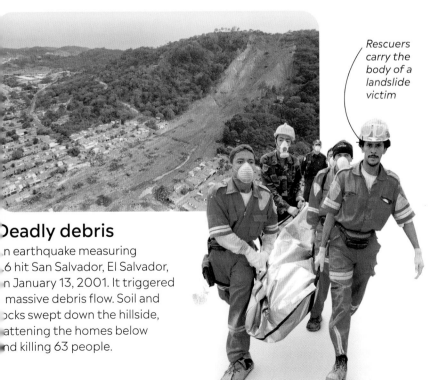

Deadly debris

n earthquake measuring
,6 hit San Salvador, El Salvador,
n January 13, 2001. It triggered
 massive debris flow. Soil and
ocks swept down the hillside,
attening the homes below
nd killing 63 people.

Slipping into the sea

The coast can be a dangerous place to build. Even solid rock cliffs can be weakened by wind and rain and eroded by pounding waves until the cliffs become overhanging. In the US, property damage due to coastal erosion costs millions of dollars every year. Breakwaters along coastlines can help prevent erosion.

Atmosphere

The atmosphere is a band of gases—mostly nitrogen, oxygen, and argon—held around Earth by gravity. Air masses move around the atmosphere, creating Earth's weather. A region's pattern of weather over time is called the climate. In some areas, extreme weather is part of the climate; in other places, where the climate is less severe, people are totally unprepared for natural disasters.

Some satellites orbit at the top of the thermosphere

Aurora, the Northern and Southern Lights, occur in the lower thermosphere

4. Thermosphere thins out into space about 400 miles (650 km) above Earth's surface

Most meteors burn up before they reach the mesosphere

3. Mesosphere extends 50 miles (80 km) above Earth's surface

2. Stratosphere reaches up to 30 miles (48 km) above Earth's surface. It contains ozone, which absorbs some of the sun's ultraviolet radiation.

1. Troposphere extends 12 miles (19 km) above Earth's surface. The weather happens here.

Atmosphere layers

The atmosphere is made up of four layers, based on temperature and humidity (the amount of water in the air). The outer layer, the thermosphere, extends into space. Gravity keeps water and air in the lowest layer, the troposphere. The sun's rays warm the air and water, causing them to move, making the weather.

Thunderclouds in the atmosphere

Viewed from space, the atmosphere looks like a light haze around Earth. In the troposphere, thunderclouds are silhouettes against the orange sun. The sky's blue is caused by sunlight interacting with gases in the air. The blue sky's layers in this picture were due to volcanic ash from Mount Pinatubo in the Philippines, and Mount Spurr in Alaska.

Soaring clouds

Clouds form in the low layer of the troposphere. Cumulonimbus storm clouds like this one can reach 15 miles (24 km) high, and punch through the top of the troposphere. Large storm clouds can hold 300,000 tons (275,000 metric tons) of water, and produce thunderstorms, hailstorms, tornadoes, torrential rain, and snow

WHAT IS WIND?

The sun warms the land and sea, which warms the air above. Warm air rises, and cold air moves in to take its place. This air movement is the wind. Prevailing winds blow steadily from one direction in circuits around the globe.

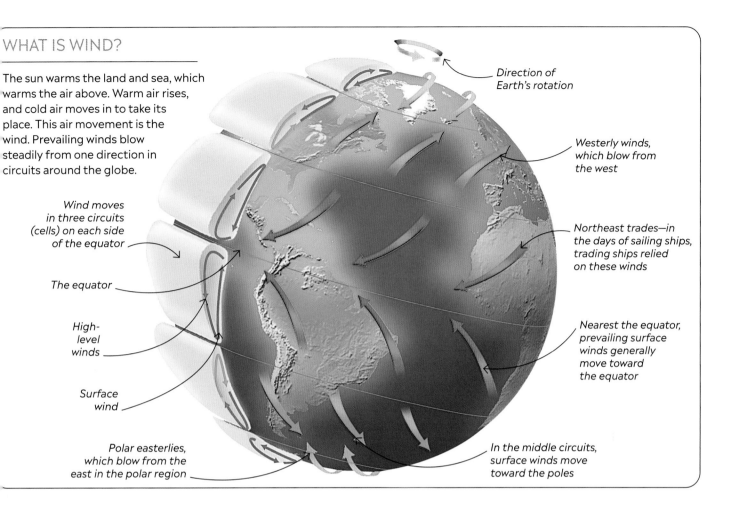

Direction of Earth's rotation

Westerly winds, which blow from the west

Northeast trades—in the days of sailing ships, trading ships relied on these winds

Nearest the equator, prevailing surface winds generally move toward the equator

Wind moves in three circuits (cells) on each side of the equator

The equator

High-level winds

Surface wind

Polar easterlies, which blow from the east in the polar region

In the middle circuits, surface winds move toward the poles

Ice storm

In North America, ice storms occur when snow melts as it falls through warm air, and then supercools as it hits cold air near the ground. The 1998 ice storm in Québec, Canada, became its most expensive natural disaster, leaving four million people without electricity. Damage caused by ice storms during the 2020–2021 North American winter cost around $30 billion.

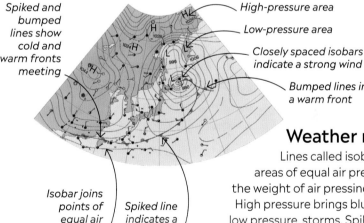

Spiked and bumped lines show cold and warm fronts meeting

High-pressure area

Low-pressure area

Closely spaced isobars indicate a strong wind

Bumped lines indicate a warm front

Isobar joins points of equal air pressure

Spiked line indicates a cold front

Weather map

Lines called isobars link areas of equal air pressure—the weight of air pressing down. High pressure brings blue skies; low pressure, storms. Spiked and bumped lines show the fronts (boundaries) of air masses. When they collide, the weather changes.

Desert dust storm

In dry desert landscapes, hot, high-pressure air sits over the land, bringing hot days and freezing nights. Occasionally, moist winds sweep across the desert, mix with the hot air, and rise high into the atmosphere, where they cool to form huge thunderclouds. The now cool, dry air falls to the ground and spreads out, creating 60-mph (100-kph) winds, which whip up dusty soil into a dust storm.

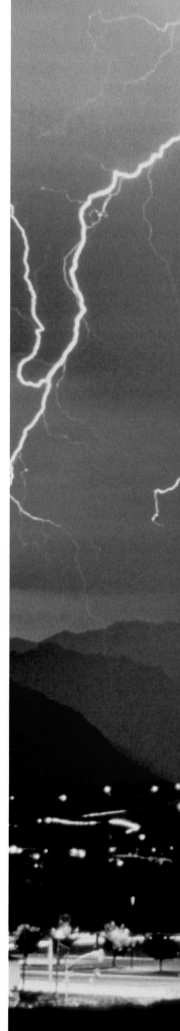

Wild weather

Eiffel Tower struck
Like other tall buildings, the Eiffel Tower in Paris, France, is protected from lightning damage by a lightning conductor—a metal cable that leads the electrical charge to the ground where it discharges harmlessly.

At any time, 2,000 thunderstorms light up the sky around the world. A bolt of lightning can reach 54,000°F (30,000°C)—five times hotter than the sun's surface—and its electrical charge can kill instantly. Most thunderstorms are in summer, when warm air rises to form thunderclouds. These storms can bring torrential rain or hail. Their paths are tracked using satellites, weather stations, and weather planes.

HOW RAIN CLOUDS FORM

The sun's heat makes water from the oceans and land evaporate. The moist, warm air rises and cools; the water vapor condenses to form water droplets. These link together into a thick cloud and fall to Earth as rain, hail, or snow. If warm, moist air rises rapidly—due to frontal wedging, mountain lifting, or converging (see diagrams)—storm clouds occur.

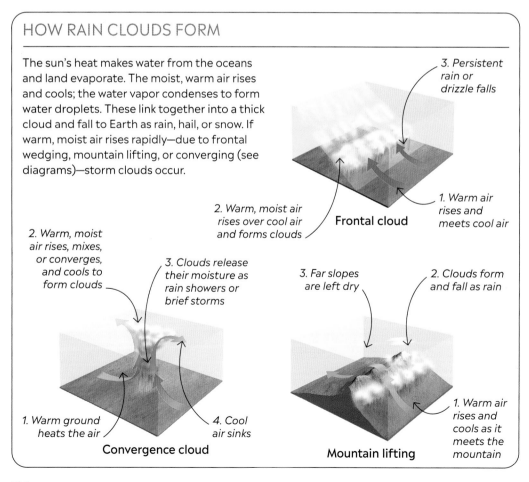

3. Persistent rain or drizzle falls

2. Warm, moist air rises over cool air and forms clouds

Frontal cloud

1. Warm air rises and meets cool air

2. Warm, moist air rises, mixes, or converges, and cools to form clouds

3. Clouds release their moisture as rain showers or brief storms

1. Warm ground heats the air

4. Cool air sinks

Convergence cloud

3. Far slopes are left dry

2. Clouds form and fall as rain

1. Warm air rises and cools as it meets the mountain

Mountain lifting

Thunder and lightning

Inside a storm cloud, water droplets and ice crystals rise and fall, building up a static electrical charge that sends a spark of lightning to the ground (fork lightning), or among the clouds (sheet lightning). The air around it heats up and expands, creating a shock wave, heard as thunder.

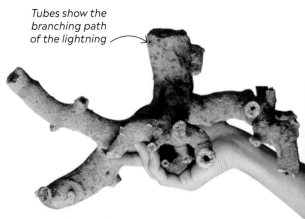

Tubes show the branching path of the lightning

Lightning sculpture

Lightning sculpted this solidified sand, called a fulgurite. As lightning passed through the sand, it heated up the grains to melting point and fused them together into hollow tubes. Lightning's heat can set trees and wooden buildings on fire.

👁 **EYEWITNESS**

Flying into the storm

US Air Force navigator Lt. Col. Mark Withee serves in the 53rd Weather Reconnaissance Squadron. He flies a special plane, called a hurricane hunter, directly into the center of severe storms. Flying through the center several times, he uses onboard sensors and radar to collect data in real time that is vital to hurricane forecasting.

Thunderclouds over Gillette, Wyoming

Black clouds and hail

Hailstones form when raindrops moving up and down in freezing black thunderclouds become coated with ice. Hailstones can be larger than baseballs, but most are pea-size. Even tiny balls of ice can damage crops and property, and turn roads into ice rinks.

Giant hailstone

Baseball

Hurricanes

Storm at sea

In late summer, above tropical seas along the equator, huge rotating storms develop. The storms—called hurricanes when they start over the Atlantic Ocean, cyclones in the Indian Ocean, and typhoons in the Pacific Ocean—can be 300–500 miles (500–800 km) across, and travel great distances. High winds, torrential rain, and surges of seawater leave a trail of destruction as they sweep inland.

Dark threat

Tropical storms are fueled by the sun's heat evaporating ocean water, which rises with the warm air to build vast storm clouds. The lifting air creates a zone of low atmospheric pressure. The surrounding air then rushes int the low-pressure zone, driving howling winds.

Hurricane forming

This satellite image from September 2004 shows spiraling clouds forming Hurricane Ivan over the Atlantic Ocean. For a hurricane to form, seawater must be warmer than 78.8°F (26°C), fueling winds of up to 73 mph (118 kph). A hurricane can pick up two billion tons of water vapor from the sea a day, to be dumped on land as potential rain.

The calm eye of the storm

INSIDE A HURRICANE

Dry air sinks into the eye of the storm

Air spirals inward at the bottom of the hurricane

Blue arrows show cool air spiraling outward at the top of the hurricane

The fastest winds and heaviest rain spiral around the low-pressure eye wall

Sea surface bulges in the low-pressure eye area

Red arrows show spiraling bands of wind and rain

A hurricane forms when an area of warm air rises above the ocean, and sucks in surrounding air. Earth's rotation makes the air spin. The spinning air rises, cools, and creates a spiral of storm clouds. A hurricane's eye is an area of calm air at its center.

Thick clouds spiral around the eye

El Niño

Every two to seven years, a weather pattern called El Niño causes winds over the Pacific to change direction. This colored satellite image shows sea temperature changes due to the 1997 El Niño event. Winds push warm water to South America, bringing tropical storms, while areas west of the ocean may suffer drought.

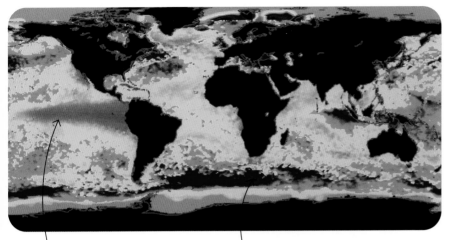

Red shows sea temperatures farthest above normal

Purple shows sea temperatures farthest below normal

Calm before the storm

The most violent part of the hurricane often follows a calm period—the sky may suddenly clear and the air grow still, as the eye of the storm passes. A few moments later, the storm returns with renewed vigor. In 2020, Hurricane Delta made landfall in Louisiana, with winds blowing at speeds of 100 mph (155 kph).

Hurricane warnings

Flags like these alert residents and ships when a hurricane is nearing the coast. Weather forecasters broadcast a "weather watch" on television, radio, and the Internet, telling people to look out for updates. Once certain the storm will strike, they issue a severe weather warning. It is best to shelter in a brick or concrete building, away from windows.

Wind and waves

In 1998, Hurricane Georges sent huge waves crashing onto the shore of Florida. When the eye passes over the coast, it brings a deadly wall of water, called a storm surge, up to 10 ft (3 m) high, caused by the eye's low air pressure.

Palm trees bend but rarely break in hurricane winds

Battling winds

Every year, about 90 hurricanes batter the world's coasts. Their wind speed and air pressure are measured to try and predict how they will develop. Satellites can spot hurricanes as they form, but accurate data comes from planes, known as hurricane hunters, sent into the hurricane. When it moves over land, a hurricane slowly runs out of energy; if it sweeps out to sea, warmth from the water can speed up the wind once more.

Cyclone Nargis

The tropical cyclone that hit Burma (Myanmar) on May 2, 2008, was the worst natural disaster in Burma's recorded history. A 13-ft (4-m) storm surge swept inland across the low-lying Irrawaddy Delta; the destructive flood waters killed 138,000 people.

Hurricane Irma over the Gulf of Mexico, September 8, 2017

Hurricane Irma over the sea, August 31, 2017

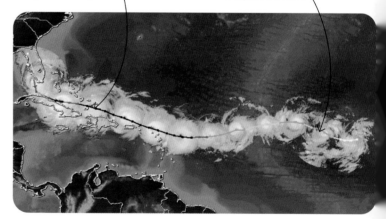

Hurricane Irma

This sequence of satellite images shows Hurricane Irma's path as it moved east to west. With winds speeds reaching 185 mph (297 kph), it wreaked havoc in the Caribbean Islands, Barbuda, and around nine states in the US. Hurricane Irma killed 47 people and displaced millions of others.

Hurricane hunters

In 1999, during a 12-hour flight into Hurricane Floyd, hurricane hunters recorded wind speed, humidity, and pressure. Weather-station computers used the data to predict Floyd's path, although hurricanes can change direction.

This infrared satellite image of Hurricane Floyd helped the hurricane hunters plan their flight.

Trail of destruction

Hurricane Michael tore through Florida in October 2018. When it made landfall in Florida, the wind speeds reached around 160 mph (257 kph)—one of the strongest landfall wind speeds recorded.

Under water

In August 2017, Hurricane Harvey hit Texas. The storm dumped more than 270 trillion gallons (102 trillion liters) of rain over the state. Some parts of the city of Houston received as much as 50 in (127 cm) of rainfall.

Trees uprooted by the force of the wind

Heavy rainfall caused extreme flooding

Great storm of '87

In the middle of an October night in 1987, a severe storm hit southern Britain. As it brewed out in the Atlantic, the storm mixed with warm winds from a hurricane. As a result, some gusts of wind reached hurricane speeds of 122 mph (196 kph), toppling 15 million trees and ruining buildings.

Hurricane
Katrina

Hurricane Katrina hit the southern US in August 2005, leaving a million people homeless, five million without power, and over 1,800 dead in the US's most destructive and costly natural disaster. Historic New Orleans lay under many feet of water; evacuees went to makeshift emergency shelters in the city and in nearby states, or moved in with relatives. Many said they were unlikely to return to the disaster-struck region.

Broken windows
Curtains dangle outside hotel windows smashed by the force of Hurricane Katrina. Beds were seen flying out of the windows of one hotel. However, some modern buildings like this one survived relatively unscathed. A commission was set up to advise the government on how best to rebuild, taking into account the needs of all citizens.

Course of Katrina
Hurricane Katrina hit the Bahamas, south Florida, Louisiana, Mississippi, and Alabama between August 23–31, 2005. Winds reached a maximum wind speed of 170 mph (273 kph), and 200 miles (320 km) of coastline suffered a storm surge. The wind finally began to lose strength 150 miles (240 km) inland, near Jackson, Mississippi.

Sousaphone is too valuable to leave behind

Storm surge
As the hurricane's eye moved across the Mississippi coast, it created a storm surge almost 33 ft (10 m) high. In the town of Long Beach, cars and rubble were swept into a towering heap against a building.

Leaving home
On August 28, Hurricane Katrina was heading for New Orleans; its mayor ordered an evacuation. With no electricity, clean water, or food supplies, the last of those able to evacuate left, bringing a few belongings.

Clear eye of the storm

Strong eyewall winds

Hurricane Katrina was one of the costliest natural disasters in the US, causing about

$106 billion

in damages.

Underwater city

Rising floodwaters breached levees (embankments) designed to protect New Orleans from flooding. One day after Katrina hit, 80 percent of the city was flooded, some areas by 20 ft (6 m) of water. It took several weeks to repair the levees and pump out the water.

Boat rescue

Thousands of New Orleans residents were left behind when the hurricane struck. Many of them gathered in evacuation centers to await rescue. After the storm, rescuers arrived in boats to pick up the people who were stranded and conducted a house-to-house search to check for survivors.

Twisting
tornadoes

The most violent winds on Earth, tornadoes (nicknamed twisters) can travel across land at speeds of 125 mph (200 kph). They can hurl around objects as large as trains, and rip roofs off houses. Tornadoes have hit almost every state in the US, but most of the world's tornadoes occur in the American Midwest's open prairies, where tornado season runs from May to October.

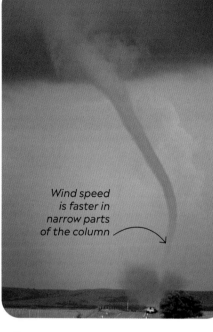

Tower of cloud called a thunderhead tops the supercell

TORNADO ALLEY

Tornado Alley, in the center of the United States, covers parts of Kansas, Oklahoma, and Missouri—the Great Plains; 80 percent of Earth's tornadoes occur here. In summer, cold air from Canada underrides warm, moist air from the Gulf of Mexico and hot, dry air from the Plains, causing atmospheric instability.

Canada

United States

Mexico

Tornado-prone areas

Flying fish

Tornadoes passing over lakes and oceans may suck up fish and frogs, then drop them on dry land.

Terrifying twister

Inside the tornado's column, air whirls inward and upward, creating a flow called a vortex, at up to 300 mph (500 kph). Low pressure inside the vortex makes the twister suck up items beneath it, like a vacuum cleaner.

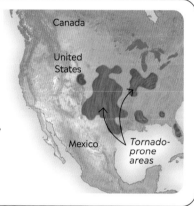

Wind speed is faster in narrow parts of the column

 EYEWITNESS

Storm chaser

American engineer Tim Samaras (1957–2013) was active in the field of researching and understanding tornadoes. He even built his own weather instruments. In 2003, his cone-shaped probe, called the turtle, was one of the first to successfully capture the conditions, including wind pressure, inside a tornado.

Tornado damage

After a tornado, the surrounding area is often flattened, with falling debris, trees snapped in two, and broken power poles. In December 2021, severe tornadoes hit the US states of Kentucky and Illinois. The unusually severe winds were some of the deadliest ever to have run through the region.

Revolving mesocyclone sucks up dust from the ground

Storm clouds

Strong winds moving in different directions in a huge, dark storm cloud (supercell) create low pressure beneath the cloud. Warm, moist air rushes into the updraft to meet cold air higher up. The two air masses turn around each other to form a wide air column—a mesocyclone.

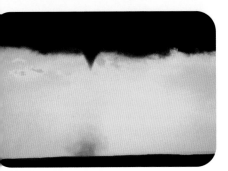

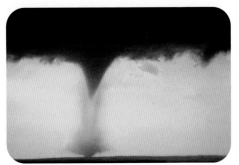

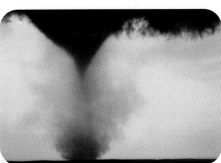

1 Funnel appears

A funnel of water vapor extends down from the cloud. As warm, moist air from the atmosphere is sucked into the mesocyclone's base, it spins upward, carrying dust with it.

2 Column forms

Warm air rises and cools, forming water vapor that joins the swirling funnel. When it touches the ground, sucking up more dust, it becomes a tornado and is clearly visible.

3 Dying down

Most tornadoes last about three minutes; the tornado slows down as it runs out of moist, warm air at the bottom or when cool, dry air sinks from the cloud.

Dust devil

As air rises in the hot desert, it can create a draft that begins to swirl, just like a tornado, picking up dust and sand. Called dust devils, they can reach 1.2 miles (2 km) high. They are less fierce than tornadoes, with winds reaching up to 60 mph (100 kph).

Waterspout

A tornado over the sea or a lake contains a column of condensed water, forming a waterspout. The wind speeds in a waterspout are usually less than those in a tornado, but the vortex could still lift a boat out of the water.

Flood **alert**

Water is vital to survival, but huge storm waves from the sea and flooding rivers make water a deadly enemy. Floods can sweep away people, animals, and poorly constructed buildings, and damage centuries-old buildings and valuable artworks. In steep landscapes, torrential rain can cause a flash flood—a surge of water that rises so rapidly it can catch people unprepared.

Rainy season

In India, children celebrate monsoon season, which starts with a thunderstorm and week-long torrential rain. Even though it brings floods, the monsoon is welcomed, as it ends the hot, humid season, and provides water for crops.

Damage caused in Rheinland-Pfalz, Germany, by the flooding of Ahr River in July 2021

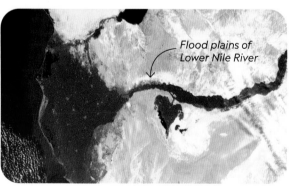

Flood plains of Lower Nile River

Fertile flood plains

Ancient Egyptians relied on the Nile's annual flooding, which naturally fertilized the flood plain (the land on either side of a river). Since 1970, the Aswan High Dam has reduced flooding; today's farmers use fertilizers instead.

Sluice gates on Three Gorges Dam, Hubei Province, China

Diverting the waters

Levels of some rivers a constantly monitored, and "sluices" channel water away from flood-prone areas. When sluice gates are open, excess water gushes into a runoff lak

THE WORLD'S RAINFALL

The average global rainfall is 40 in (1,000 mm) a year. But this is not evenly distributed. The amount of rain an area receives depends on factors such as air temperature, land shape and size, and the season.

■ More than 97 in (2,474 mm)
■ 19–97 in (474–2,474 mm)
□ Less than 19 in (474 mm)

High tides threaten low-lying cities in northern Europe

River floods in south-eastern US

Amazon River bursts its banks annually

Storm floods likely on Pacific coast

Wet-season floods can affect central Africa

Monsoons cause flooding around Bay of Bengal

Tropical storms can cause flooding in northern Australia

North America
Atlantic Ocean
Pacific Ocean
South America
Europe
Asia
Africa
Indian Ocean
Australia

Map showing the annual amount of rainfall around the world

Inland flooding

In the summer of 2021, a large and intense storm passed over parts of northern Europe with devastating effects. In Germany, there were nearly 200 deaths from flooding—this was the worst natural disaster for over half a century. More than 15,000 service personnel were involved in the search and rescue.

Pond formed by melted ice (meltwater)

Melting glacier

The slow melting of frozen river ice or mountain glaciers do not generally cause a flood, but floating chunks of melting ice can form a dam across the river, causing an overflow upstream. When the ice dam cracks, the released water causes a flash flood.

rotecting London

dal rivers, such as the Thames, are risk from storm surges and floods ue to unusually high tides. The Thames arrier's gates close to prevent tidal rges from traveling upriver, otecting London.

Gates open to let river traffic through

Doppler radar dome receives returning radio waves

Colors on the radar indicate the amount of rainfall with red meaning the most intense

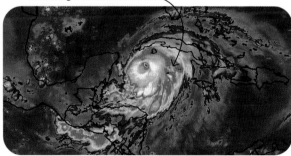

Severe weather warnings

Doppler radar equipment makes accurate weather forecasts. It locates storms and measures their speed and direction by bouncing radio waves off clouds. This Doppler radar image shows Hurricane Ivan from 2004.

Raging waters

When a flood strikes , roads become impassable, either too deep in water for vehicles to travel, or washed away by the floodwaters. With no way to escape the flood, people climb higher and higher as the waters rise, first to the upper stories of buildings, then onto roofs or in high trees. There, they wait for rescuers to arrive in boats or helicopters. One way to protect people from the danger of flooding would be to stop building settlements on flood plains. But many large cities already exist on flood plains. In heavily populated, low-lying countries, such as Bangladesh and the Netherlands, there is not enough higher ground.

Noah's ark
In the Bible story, Noah's ark floated on a flood caused by 40 days of heavy rain. Noah and his passengers stayed on the ark for a year until the floodwaters dried up.

Ball of smoking incense

The right rain
Rain has always been vital for crops—and storms destructive. The Mayans hoped Chac, their god of rain, would provide rain but keep floods at bay.

The usual course of the Yangtze River

Houses under 3 ft (1m) of water

Controlling the Yangtze River
The banks of China's Yangtze River burst regularly after heavy rain, killing thousands of people in some years. One of the worst floods occurred in August 2002, when some 900,000 people were displaced. In 1994, the Chinese government had begun work on the Three Gorges Dam (the world's largest dam), designed to control the flooding. The dam itself was finished in 2006.

Container for emergency food ration

Rescue worker helps a woman climb down from her roof into a boat

Escaping the water

People climbed onto roofs and trees to escape the 1993 Mississippi floods. About 45 people died and nearly 70,000 were left homeless.

Living with floods

Bangladeshi women and children line up, waist-deep in floodwater, for emergency supplies. Bangladeshi people are accustomed to flooding every year during the monsoon. But in 1997–1998, the weather pattern called El Niño triggered such a huge increase in the monsoon rain that two-thirds of the country was inundated. Ten million people lost their homes.

Road to nowhere

This collapsed bridge in Quincy, Illinois, was submerged when the United States' largest river, the Mississippi, and its tributary, the Missouri, flooded in 1993. The floods occurred when dams and levees burst following ten times the usual amount of spring rainfall on the central plains.

Swirling waters

In southeastern Australia, cars sit in floodwater after heavy rain in September 2010. The state of Victoria suffered its worst floods in a decade, forcing cities to evacuate and cutting the electricity to 40,000 homes. Within three months, more floods devastated the state of Queensland.

Aerial view of swamped cars near Wangaratta, Australia

Drought

It is hard to tell when a drought starts, but a drought is well underway when rivers run dry. It may cause a famine, and people and animals starve. The best preparation is to store water when it is plentiful, but the driest places never have enough water. In such places, drought cannot be prevented—but famine can, as long as water, food, and aid reach people in time.

Boat grounded on sands that were once under the Aral Sea

Vanishing sea
Since 1997, the Aral Sea between Kazakhstan and Uzbekistan has shrunk to only 10 percent of its size. It has become more salty, too, killing the fish that lived there. There have been various attempts to replenish the sea, but most have failed.

Field of dried-out sunflowers in Spain

Thirsty crops
In a drought, crops such as these sunflowers die, and the farmers suffer losses. In wealthy countries, watering bans may occur, but there is usually enough water in reservoirs for drinking and washing until rain replenishes water supplies.

Underground water
During a drought, soil and surface water dry up, but groundwater flows deep underground, trapped by hard layers of rock. Deep wells tap into this. In 2003, Gujarat in India suffered its worst drought in 10 years. People traveled far to deep wells, often on foot, and waited their turn to get water.

Holding back the desert
During droughts, sand dunes can spread, burying nearby towns and farms. To stop this, some farmers plant millet crops in the dunes to bind the sand together and stop it from blowing to the fields.

Dust Bowl

In the 1930s, intensive farming ruined the soil in the Great Plains of the United States. When drought struck, the soil turned to dust and blew away. Crop failures and famine followed. Half a million people abandoned their farms.

Burial mounds

Animal carcass, a common sight during severe droughts

Famine

When drought hit Ethiopia and Sudan in 1984–1985, crops failed, and then livestock starved. As a result, the people had no food and no income to buy any, and they, too, starved. In the famine that followed, 450,000 died.

Brick lining stops soil from collapsing into the well

Metal pots lowered on ropes to reach groundwater

Refugee camp

In the worst droughts, people have to gather in refugee camps, like this one in Mogadishu, Somalia, to receive food and shelter. Aid organizations, such as Oxfam and Médecins Sans Frontières (Doctors Without Borders), supply clean water, food, medicines, and shelter.

Wildfire

From the first flicker of flame in dry grass, a wildfire spreads rapidly. Also known as bush fires or forest fires, wildfires regularly occur during the long, dry summers in Australia, California, and southern Europe. Some are left to burn out, and the landscape regenerates naturally. When a wildfire is out of control, firefighters battle to stop it destroying whole forests or spreading to built-up areas.

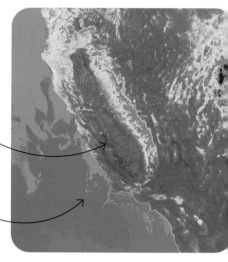

Dark red areas are the hottest, showing ground temperatures above 131°F (55°C)

Cool blue-green area is the Pacific Ocean

Heatwave

This thermal satellite image shows temperatures in California in May 2004 when a heatwave led to an early wildfire season. In hot years, little rain dries out vegetation, making it easier to set alight and harder to stop a wildfire.

Thick, choking smoke rises from a land-clearance fire

Farmers' fires

In Southeast Asia and South America, farmers clear rainforest by burning it down. They grow crops on the land for a few years and then let it become forest again. Farmers' fires are difficult to control, and they sometimes grow into dangerous wildfires.

Lightning bolt

About half of all wildfires are started by people; the rest start naturally. The spark that lights most natural fires is lightning. Dry plants in summer provide the fuel, and storm winds fan the flames. Within minutes, an area can be transformed.

Black Saturday

In early 2009, a series of wildfires struck southeastern Australia, starting on Saturday, February 7. The fires killed 173 people in total—the worst-ever death toll from wildfire in Australia. The day when they started is now known as Black Saturday. Wildfires occur regularly in many part of the world and are linked to high temperatures, low humidity, and strong winds. Their incidence and severity are on the rise due to global warming.

- Indian Ocean
- Island of Borneo
- Smoke from wildfires
- Red dots show fires still burning

New growth

Wildfires are vital to North American lodgepole pines, which only release seeds in a fire's heat. Forest fires also clear land for new seedlings, return nutrients to soil, and kill pests and diseases.

An island burns

In the summer of 2002, fires and smoke in Borneo, Southeast Asia, were visible from space. Logging companies started the fires to clear rainforest, but they soon got out of control, destroying an area half the size of Switzerland. Even after a rainforest fire is put out, the peat under the forest smolders and can reignite flames.

Rising hot air sucks in more air at the bottom, fueling the fire with oxygen

More than
980,000 acres
(400,000 hectares) of land was burned down during the Black Saturday bushfires.

Fighting fires

It may take a week to bring a wildfire under control. In remote areas, firefighters battle leaping flames, falling trees, choking smoke, and 932°F (500°C) heat. But some wildfires are unstoppable; in 1997, after months of drought, 100 fires blazed in Indonesia's rainforests. Firefighting experts could not bring the fires under control. The monsoon rains finally fell, killing the flames until the next wildfire season.

Helicopter carries one pilot, two fire captains, and eight firefighters

Fire truck

In urban areas, fire engine hoses can connect to fire hydrants for water. In the wilderness, tanks of water are driven to the scene of the fire, or pumped from nearby water sources.

Sparks shoot out as the tree ignites

Health worker hands masks to a commuter

Flaming tree

Natural oils in Australian *Eucalyptus* trees stop them from drying out in the arid climate, but make them very flammable. In the hot, dry summer, the heat of a nearby fire can make the trees ignite spontaneously. After the fire, new growth can spring from beneath the charred bark, and the fire-resistant seeds germinate in the ash-rich soil.

Choking smog

In 1997, the smoke from the raging forest fires in Southeast Asia created a gray haze of choking smog that affected 70 million people. Many people wore protective masks in an attempt to try and minimize damage to the lungs.

Fighting fires

Firefighters spray water or chemicals onto burning vegetation to lower its heat and make it less flammable. They may cut down or burn vegetation where the fire is heading so that it runs out of fuel. They may also create wide trenches that flames cannot leap over.

Cruise speed is 126 mph (203 kph)

Tank can hold 360 gallons (1,360 liters) of water or foam

Water turned to steam by the heat of the flames

There were

8,600 wildfires
across California in 2021.

Dousing the flames

Wildfires are an annual hazard to people living near forested areas of southern California. The local fire service has helicopters that scoop or suck up water from a lake, and dump it on the fire or surrounding vegetation to make it less likely to catch fire. In 2021, fires spread across nearly 2,570,000 acres (640,000 hectares) of the state.

Smoke jumpers

In remote areas, firefighters parachute in to tackle small fires before they spread. They cannot parachute with much, so equipment is dropped separately. Afterward, they often have to hike out of the area carrying the pumps and tools.

High collar protects neck from branches during jump

Helmet with heavy mesh face mask

Gear

Bleached coral has no algae

Undamaged coral

Climate change

Over millions of years, Earth's climate has swung between ice ages and hot periods. Long-term climate change is due to shifts in Earth's tilt, heat from the sun, and the distance between the sun and Earth. Earth has been growing warmer for the last 100 years, but the recent rate of change has greatly increased. Most scientists believe this global warming is due to polluting gases from fossil fuels, agriculture, and change in land use, and that it will probably cause more extreme weather.

Bleached coral

Rising global temperatures are warming the oceans, threatening tropical coral reefs. A 1.8°F (1°C) rise can make coral eject the plantlike algae that live in their tissues and supply them with food. This makes coral turn white, and ultimately it may die.

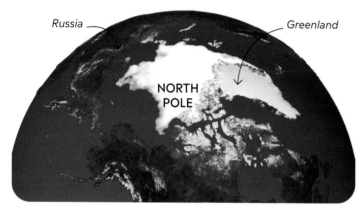

Russia

Greenland

NORTH POLE

Arctic Sea ice, 1979

One effect of global warming is the reduced sea ice in the Arctic. This satellite image shows the ice sheet that covered Greenland, and sea ice that stretched as far as the north coast of Russia.

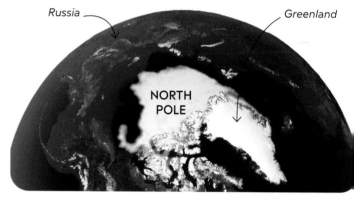

Russia

Greenland

NORTH POLE

Arctic Sea ice, 2020

This satellite image shows how the summer sea ice shrank in 2020. Scientists think it could melt completely by 2035. The Greenland ice sheet's fringes are thinning, and extra meltwater has raised sea levels, threatening low-lying islands and coasts.

Polar habitat under threat

Reduced sea ice threatens the survival of polar bears because they spend much of their lives traveling across the ice, hunting for seals in the Arctic waters. Warmer conditions in the Arctic may mean that most of the floating ice will become seasonal, melting in summer and reforming in winter.

EARTH'S TILT

The seasons are created by Earth's tilt; areas that point toward the sun receive more heat. This tilt angle changes over many years; the greater the tilt, the greater the seasonal difference. When this coincides with changes in Earth's orbit, taking it closer to or farther from the sun, its temperature can vary enough to cause an ice age or raise temperatures.

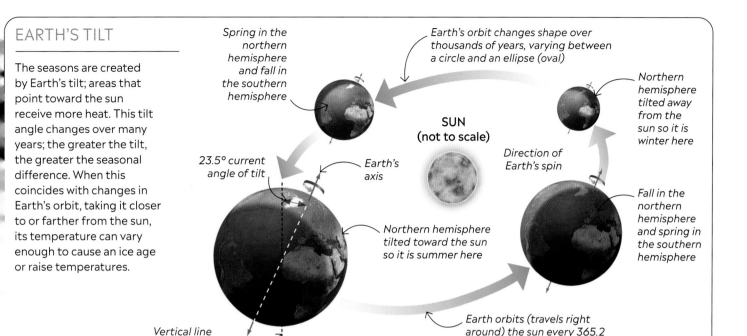

Spring in the northern hemisphere and fall in the southern hemisphere

Earth's orbit changes shape over thousands of years, varying between a circle and an ellipse (oval)

Northern hemisphere tilted away from the sun so it is winter here

SUN (not to scale)

Direction of Earth's spin

23.5° current angle of tilt

Earth's axis

Northern hemisphere tilted toward the sun so it is summer here

Fall in the northern hemisphere and spring in the southern hemisphere

Vertical line through Earth

Earth orbits (travels right around) the sun every 365.2 days, or roughly once a year

---

 EYEWITNESS

Predicting the future
Scientist Dr. Robert Mulvaney leads a team at the British Antarctic Survey that drills and studies ice cores (as seen below) from the Arctic, Greenland, and Antarctica. The ice is a record of the climate over 100,000 years and more. His team studies the effects of climate change on polar ice sheets and aims to predict sea level rises.

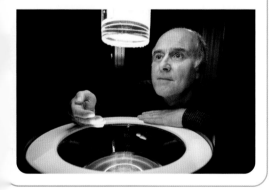

Hollow drill pipe for extracting ice core

Learning from the past
Geologists drill samples called cores from the ancient ice deep inside the Antarctic ice sheet. These reveal data about surface temperatures over thousands of years, as the ice sheet developed. Ice cores can show how much carbon dioxide, volcanic ash, dust, and pollen used to exist in the atmosphere. Studying how climate and atmosphere have changed may help us predict how it will change in the future.

Drifting chunks of ice melt faster than the solid ice sheet

Exploitation

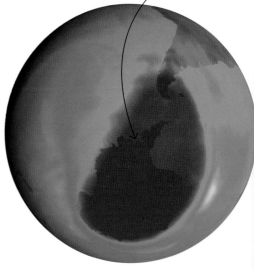

Reduced ozone over Antarctica

Some disasters are due to our exploitation of nature. Waste fumes from cars or industry pollute the air. Burning fossil fuels provides us with power, but it also releases climate-changing gases. Forests are cut down for timber and farming; oceans are overfished. Scientists warn that we need to cut our use of natural resources and our production of pollution.

Pollution monitor

Poisoning the air

Like many cities on hot days, Santiago, Chile, is buried in smog—a sooty fog of harmful gases, including carbon monoxide, produced when vehicle exhaust fumes react with sunlight. The polluted air can aggravate breathing conditions and cause eye irritations.

Thinning ozone

A layer of ozone gas forms in the atmosphere when oxygen reacts with sunlight, blocking some of the sun's harmful radiation. Gases called CFCs, used in refrigerators and aerosols react with oxygen and thin the ozone layer, allowing through more of the sun's rays. CFCs are now banned in many countries.

Deforestation

Forests are being cut down faster than they are replaced. Trees provide timber, and cleared land can be used for farming. But forests are vital to life on Earth; trees absorb carbon dioxide, and produce oxygen. Woodlands act as a carbon store—removing them increases the level of carbon dioxide in the atmosphere.

In China, people flee a dust storm caused by desertification

Desertification

On desert edges, years can go by with little rainfall. When the edges are heavily populated, vegetation is stripped, usually for animal feed, faster than it can grow. Soon desertification, the spread of the desert, turns soil to dust. In Asia and Africa, millions of poor people are losing land and livelihoods as deserts spread.

Gray areas show coral damaged by dynamite

Blast fishing

Coral reefs are being damaged by blasting fish out of the water with dynamite. In parts of the developing world, blast fishing is a cheap, quick way to fish, but it kills the coral beneath the waters. It can take more than 20 years before the coral begins to recover.

Acid rain

These trees have been killed by acid rain. Burning fossil fuels releases gases that form acids in the atmosphere. The wind carries the acids far from the places that produced them, until they fall as acid rain, killing trees and poisoning rivers.

Dwindling resources

Factory trawlers like this catch many tons of fish a day. Globally, fish count for 10 percent of our protein intake. As our population grows, so does the demand for fish, and stocks are falling rapidly around the world.

Catch of herring on a Norwegian trawler

Infectious
diseases

The world's deadliest disasters are caused by microorganisms—such as bacteria, fungi, and viruses—which invade the body through cuts, food and drink, insect bites, and the air we breathe. They cause infectious diseases—including malaria, cholera, and AIDS—which account for more than 13 million deaths each year. Some can even kill by destroying the crops we depend on for food.

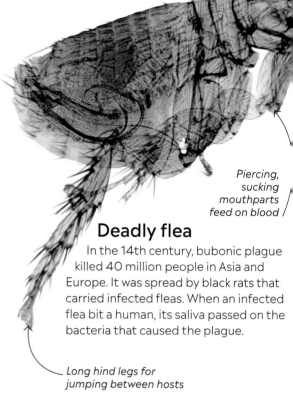

Piercing, sucking mouthparts feed on blood

Deadly flea

In the 14th century, bubonic plague killed 40 million people in Asia and Europe. It was spread by black rats that carried infected fleas. When an infected flea bit a human, its saliva passed on the bacteria that caused the plague.

Long hind legs for jumping between hosts

Viruses

This scanning electron micrograph shows the variola virus that causes smallpox. A virus is a package of genetic material (the instructions for cells) with a protein shell. It invades a host's cells and then injects its own genetic material into the cell, giving it the disease.

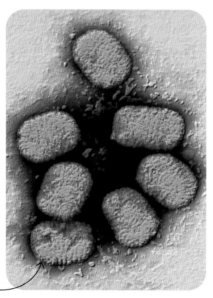

Protein coat locks on to host cell, allowing it to be invaded

Power of the microscope

Scientists can study disease-causing microorganisms using microscopes. A transmission electron microscope (TEM), such as this one, can magnify objects up to 2 million times. Dutch scientist Anton van Leeuwenhoek (1632-1723) was the first to observe tiny living organisms such as bacteria under a microscope.

Air rushes from the lungs at 93 mph (150 kph)

Infectious droplets

Disease-carrying organisms can be spread in water droplets from a sneeze. The common cold, smallpox, and tuberculosis are all spread this way.

otato blight

ungi are tiny, plantlike organisms that feed
plants and animals. This scanning electron
icroscope image shows *Phytophthora
festans*—a fungus that rots potatoes with
otato blight. It ruined potato crops in Europe
the 1840s, starving a million people in Ireland
here potatoes were the main food.

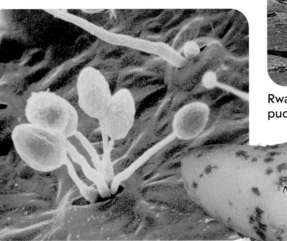

Rwandan refugees skim a mud
puddle for their drinking water

*Potato blight
mold spot*

Dirty water

After a disaster, refugees in camps have
limited clean water, making cholera a big
threat. Caused by bacteria that thrive in
dirty water, it causes diarrhea and vomiting,
which can lead to severe dehydration.

Smallpox scarring

This Nigerian statue of the Spirit of
Smallpox is covered in spots—the
smallpox rash. Smallpox is no longer a
threat, but was highly infectious. It left
unsightly scars—if people were lucky
enough to survive. There was no
treatment for it.

Pandemic

A disease that spreads rapidly among people is known as an epidemic. When it affects vast numbers over a wide area, it is a pandemic. In 2019, a flu-like virus spread across the world. Named coronavirus (COVID-19), it was declared a pandemic in March 2020. The spread of an illness can be averted by killing the disease-carrying organisms, such as mosquitoes; others, by vaccination and health education. Outbreaks of waterborne diseases like cholera can be stopped as long as people have access to clean water.

Flu research

The 1918–1920 influenza (flu) pandemic killed 25–50 million people worldwide. Researchers hope to isolate the flu virus from these sample blocks, which contain lung and brain tissue from victims, to discover why this flu strain was so deadly. Flu viruses are hard to treat because they can change form.

Names of victims of the flu pandemic

Vaccinating the world

In 2020, scientists around the world worked urgently to develop COVID-19 vaccines, with several approved by the year's end. A vaccination stimulates the body's immune system to build up resistance against a specific infection. In December 2020, mass vaccination began against COVID-19. By December 2021, more than a year after a pandemic was declared, about 270 million cases had been reported.

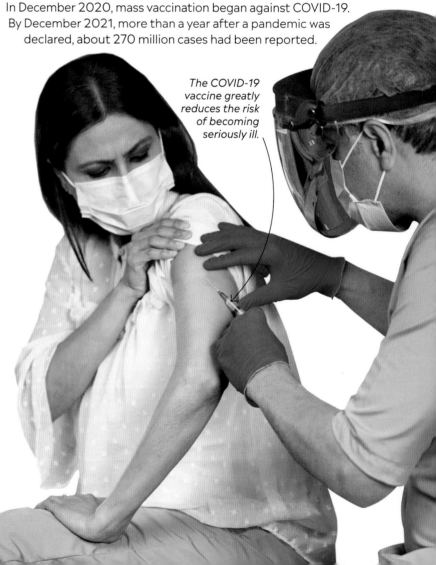

The COVID-19 vaccine greatly reduces the risk of becoming seriously ill.

Plague outbreak

In 1994, pneumonic plague—which affects the lungs, but is caused by the same bacteria as glandular bubonic plague—killed 51 in Surat, western India. Street trash was burned to destroy the disease-carrying rats.

Controlling malaria

Mosquito eggs hatch into larvae in water, and then develop into adults. Adult females feed on mammal blood, spreading diseases such as malaria and dengue fever. Scientists have not yet found a way to prevent mosquitoes from breeding, so mosquito larvae are killed to help prevent the spread of these diseases.

Infection control

Hygiene is key in the fight against lethal microorganisms, which thrive in dirty conditions. Some, such as MRSA (methicillin-resistant *Staphylococcus aureus*), have grown a resistance to most antibiotics, so treating them is difficult.

AIDS educators

Candles are lit on World AIDS day for victims, as campaigners try to educate people to prevent its spread. There is no cure for AIDS, and many do not have access to drugs that can control it.

Vaccines for all

COVAX is a global initiative that aims to gives everyone in every nation a chance to have the COVID-19 vaccine. COVAX supports the research, development, and manufacturing of vaccines, and negotiates costs, to ensure 190 countries receive vaccines. Shown here is a batch of vaccines being offloaded at an airport in Somalia.

White blood cell, colored green in this image

HIV, colored red, invades a blood cell

HIV and AIDS

The Human Immunodeficiency Virus (HIV), which causes AIDS (Acquired Immune Deficiency Syndrome), kills white blood cells, multiplies, and spreads. As more blood cells are destroyed, the body cannot fight infection. More than 37 million people have HIV, and AIDS is becoming one of the biggest killers in history.

← *Mount Vesuvius*

The future

As Earth's population grows, disasters will cause greater loss of life. The area affected may also be greater. In the future, scientists fear a huge volcanic eruption in the US, and a mega-tsunami from the Canary Islands. In our lifetimes, a global pandemic is a more likely disaster, but a Near Earth Object (NEO) crashing into our planet could wipe out all life in a single blow.

Devastation of Italy

If Mount Vesuvius exploded today, the effect would be devastating. Southern Italy is the most densely populated high-risk volcanic area on Earth. Naples, which has a million people, would be one of six urban areas in danger.

Supervolcano

Below Yellowstone National Park, a massive magma chamber heats water that bursts from geysers. If enough pressure built up in the chamber, the resulting volcanic eruption could destroy the US and blast enough ash into the air to cool Earth. Scientists warn that a Yellowstone eruption is overdue.

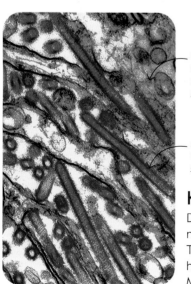

Culture cells used in virus research shown in blue

Influenza virus particles shown in red

Going global

Poultry workers in China were careful to avoid getting bird flu. It is usually spread by birds, but can grow a strain that spreads between people, just like swine flu, which killed 100 million in 1918–1919. Existing vaccines do not work on new strains, and so infected travelers could cause a global pandemic.

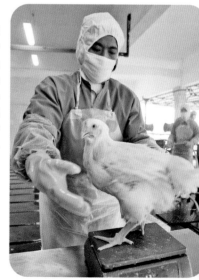

Killer flu

Diseases that develop strains capable of infecting more than one species can become very potent. The poultry disease, avian influenza (bird flu), infected humans in Hong Kong, China, in 1997. In 2009 in Mexico, swine (pig) flu also infected humans.

The 10½-ft (3.2-m) infrared telescope is located near the Mauna Kea summit in Hawaii.

The Cumbre Vieja ridge could collapse

Mega-tsunami

Some scientists think a volcanic eruption could cause half of the Canary Island of La Palma to collapse. The 500-billion-ton landslide would send a mega-tsunami to engulf the east coast of the US with 65-ft- (20-m-) high waves.

Tracking skies

Telescopes, such as the NASA Infrared Telescope Facility (IRTF) in Hawaii can track NEOs that could collide with Earth. NASA keeps track of over 12,000 NEOs— none of them heading for Earth just yet. A ½-mile- (1-km-) wide NEO would flatten a 300-mile (500-km) area.

Collision course

Evidence suggests that 66 million years ago, a 6-mile- (10-km-) wide object hit Mexico's Yucatán Peninsula, producing a mega-tsunami, with waves over ½ mile (1km) high. A dust-filled cloud rose into the atmosphere, blocking out the sun and creating a long global winter. It is thought that this caused the extinction of the dinosaurs and two-thirds of other animal species. To protect Earth from future NEOs, scientists are searching for ways to destroy them, or to push them off course.

Artist's impression of the asteroid or comet strike that destroyed the dinosaurs

Did you **know?**

AMAZING FACTS

So many volcanoes occur around the Pacific Plate that this zone is known as the Ring of Fire.

The first crater recognized as being created by an asteroid impact was Meteor Crater in Arizona. Before this, people thought it was the remains of an ancient volcano.

Forest fires clear trees and shrubs from the ground, giving the fresh seedlings of California's giant sequoias the space and sunlight they need to grow.

The mature sequoia's thick, spongy bark protects the trunk from burning, and its deep roots reach water far underground. It's no wonder some of these trees live to be 3,000 years old.

Burned giant sequoia, California

Rain may fall once in eight years in the Sahara Desert.

Seismograms detect more than a million quakes each year. Only about 150,000 are noticeable.

Tsunamis were once called seismic sea waves, as it was thought they were caused only by earthquakes. Water surface impacts can also trigger them, so the name tsunami, meaning harbor wave, is used.

A tree's inner moisture boils if lightning strikes it, blowing it apart.

Thunder is the sound of air around a bolt of lightning exploding as it is heated to 54,000°F (30,000°C) in less than a second.

For a hurricane to develop over the sea, the sea temperature must be no lower than 80°F (27°C).

In January 1974, a tornado in McComb, Mississippi, threw three buses over a 6-ft- (1.8-m-) high wall.

In December 1952, 4,000 people died in London's coal-driven smog.

From 1550–1850 there were fewer sun spots and solar flares on the sun, which gave out less heat. On Earth, this was a cooler period called the Little Ice Age.

The 2004 Asian tsunami washed away sand that had buried a 1,200-year-old city at Mahabalipuram, India.

Above Antarctica, the seasonal hole in the ozone layer peaked at 11.3 million sq miles (29.2 million sq km) in 2000. It is getting smaller.

Conditions for drought vary, depending on how much rain is normal and the season. In the US, a drought is 21 days with less than 30 percent normal rainfall; in the Sahara, it is two years without rain.

If out in the open during a tornado, lie down in a low-lying area with your hands over your head until it passes.

Rain darkens the desert sands

The oldest land rocks are 3.5 billion years old, the oldest ocean rocks are just 200 million years old—because new seafloor is added as plates pull apart, and old seafloor is subducted elsewhere.

Ozone gas would damage your lungs if breathed, but the ozone layer is vital to filter harmful radiation.

The northern hemisphere has more quakes than the southern.

When the Xiangjiang River in China flooded homes in August 2002, some residents in Changsha had to live on a bridge's staircase. The only way people could get around was by boat.

Flooding in Changsha, China

On December 26, 2004, a 10-year-old British girl saw the water recede at Maikhao Beach, Phuket, Thailand. Remembering her school geography lessons, she realized that a tsunami was about to happen. She warned people and saved 100 lives.

QUESTIONS AND ANSWERS

How far can lightning travel?

More than 6 miles (10 km). If a storm is elsewhere, you may still be struck.

How are hurricane names decided?

Each hurricane begins with the next alphabet letter. Male and female names alternate. After a fatal one, the name is dropped. Typhoons are named differently.

How are avalanche survivors found?

Teams of rescuers probe the snow with long sticks. If it meets an obstruction, they dig to see if someone is buried. Some skiers carry devices that signal to rescuers in an avalanche.

Searching for avalanche survivors in Switzerland, 2002

What is smog?

Smog is a mixture of smoke and fog. It is worst when pollutants are in low, cold air under a warmer-air lid. Cities surrounded by hills suffer smog, as low-level air is sheltered from winds and a warm-air lid can settle over it.

How did scientists figure out that continents move around Earth?

In 1915, German scientist Alfred Wegener noticed that the South American continent would fit against Africa's west side. He stated that the continents were once a single landmass. It took 30 years for this to be accepted.

Which pandemic led to the highest number of fatalities?

The 1918–1920 influenza pandemic killed 25–50 million worldwide.

Is it possible to harness the energy of a volcano?

Volcanoes are a source of renewable energy. In volcanically active countries such as Iceland, geothermal power stations pump water into Earth's crust. Hot magma turns it to steam, which rises and turns turbines for electricity.

Erupting volcano

In which direction do tornadoes spin?

Tornadoes spin counterclockwise in the northern hemisphere, and clockwise in the southern.

Storm waves caused by El Niño strike Malibu, California, in 1983

Why is the weather pattern which switches water currents in the Pacific called El Niño?

The weather pattern normally occurs around Christmas, and El Niño means "Christ Child" in Spanish.

RECORD BREAKERS

HEAVIEST HAILSTONES: In 1986, huge hailstones weighing more than 2 lb (1 kg) fell in Gopalganj, Bangladesh.

MOST ACTIVE VOLCANO: Kilauea in Hawaii has been erupting continuously since 1983, making it the most active volcano.

MOST EXPENSIVE NATURAL DISASTER: The 2011 Japanese tsunami is the most costly.

LONGEST LASTING CYCLONE: In 1994, Hurricane John formed over the Pacific Ocean. It traveled over a distance of 8,250 miles (13,280 km) and lasted 31 days.

FASTEST AVALANCHE: In 1980, Mount St. Helens erupted in the US, triggering a 250-mph (400-kph) avalanche.

Timeline

This timeline outlines some of the most devastating natural disasters in history. From the earliest times, scientists and inventors have studied and attempted to predict them. Some of their discoveries are cataloged here, too.

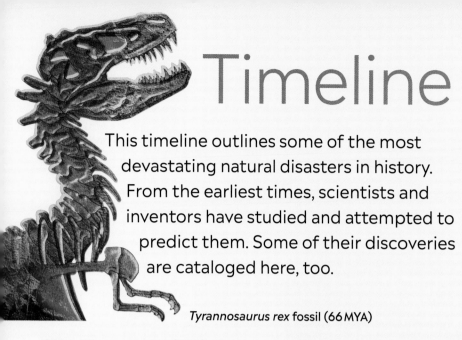

Tyrannosaurus rex fossil (66 MYA)

250 million years ago (MYA) The largest mass extinction in history saw 90 percent of all living organisms die out. Scientists cannot find the cause, but volcanic eruptions in Siberia may have altered the climate worldwide.

66 MYA A massive asteroid or comet hits the Yucatán Peninsula, Mexico, generating a mega-tsunami that plays its part in wiping out two-thirds of all species, including dinosaurs.

c. 2200 BCE Records suggest that the city of Troy, in modern Turkey, was hit by a meteor shower that set fire to the city and killed most of its people.

c. 1640 BCE The island of Santorini in the Mediterranean erupts, causing a tsunami that destroys the Minoan civilization on Crete. Many people link this event with the legend of Atlantis.

79 CE In Italy, the eruption of Mount Vesuvius destroys the towns of Pompeii and Herculaneum.

132 CE In China, Zhang Heng invents the first earthquake detector.

1348 Black Death, or bubonic plague, arrives in Europe from the east. It kills 40 million people—a quarter of Europe's population.

Black Death, London (1348)

1441 Concerned about the lives of peasants working the land, King Sejong of Korea orders the development of a rain gauge to forecast floods and droughts.

1492-1900 Ninety percent of the Indigenous peoples of the Americas die, many as a result of infectious diseases, such as smallpox, brought to the continent by Europeans.

1556 On January 3, the most destructive earthquake in recorded history hits Shaanxi province, China, killing 800,000 people. Many of the victims are buried alive.

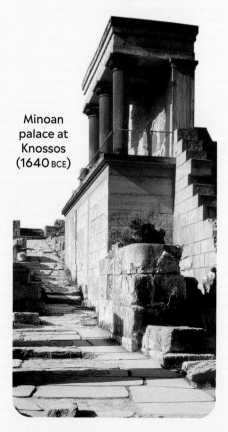

Minoan palace at Knossos (1640 BCE)

1703 Edo (now Tokyo), Japan, is destroyed by an earthquake and tsunami that kills 200,000 people.

1752 Dangerous experiments with electricity by Benjamin Franklin will eventually lead to the invention of the lightning conductor.

Benjamin Franklin's lightning experiment, 1752

1755 Triggered by an earthquake, a tsunami hits Lisbon, Portugal, with waves 50 ft (15 m) high and kills 60,000 people.

1792 An avalanche of debris from the side of Mount Unzen near Nagasaki, Japan, creates a tsunami that kills more than 14,000 people.

1798 English doctor Edward Jenner develops the first vaccine, against smallpox.

1815 Mount Tambora blows apart Sumbawa island, Indonesia, in the largest eruption in recorded history. The dust and gas produced affect the global climate, and 1815 becomes known as the Year Without a Summer.

1840s Potato blight destroys potato crops throughout Europe, bringing widespread famine. In Ireland, most people rely on potatoes for food and more than a million die.

1851-1866 China's Yellow and Yangtze rivers flood repeatedly over the land between them known as the Rice Bowl. Up to 50 million people drown.

1860s Weather-observing stations are set up around the world to make accurate weather forecasts.

64 Inspired by Swiss philanthropist ...enri Dunant, the International ...ommittee of the Red Cross, the ...st international aid organization, ...founded in Geneva, Switzerland.

874-1876 Measles is brought to Fiji, ...olynesia, by Europeans and kills ...ne-third of its Indigenous people.

882-1883 German scientist Robert ...och identifies the bacteria that ...ause cholera and tuberculosis.

883 Eruption of the volcanic island ...Krakatau (Krakatoa), Indonesia, ...uses a tsunami that kills 36,000 ...eople in Java and Sumatra.

885 British geologist John ...ilne invents the first modern ...eismograph for measuring ...arth tremors.

900 In the worst local natural ...saster in US history, a ...urricane and storm ...urge kill more than ...000 people in ...alveston, Texas.

1902 On May 8, Mount Pelée in Martinique, erupts. It leaves only two survivors out of 30,000 in St. Pierre, and causes a tsunami in the Caribbean.

1906 The Great San Francisco Earthquake is estimated to have killed nearly 3,000 people. Fires follow and burn the mostly wooden city. New buildings have to conform to quake safety regulations.

1908 A possible comet explodes before impact near Tunguska, in a remote region of northern Russia. The huge blast flattens 850 sq miles (2,200 sq km) of forest, but no deaths are recorded in this largely unpopulated area.

TransAmerica earthquake-proof skyscraper, San Francisco, 1972

1911 On January 31, on Luzon island in the Philippines, the Ta'al volcano obliterates 13 villages and towns. Most of the 1,335 victims choke on ash and sulfur dioxide.

1917-1918 Influenza epidemic kills 25–50 million people worldwide.

1921-1922 A drought and civil war devastate the region of Volga, Russia, causing widespread famine. More than 20 million people are affected.

1923 The Great Kanto Earthquake hits Tokyo, Japan, killing 140,000 people and destroying 360,000 buildings.

1930s Droughts along with poor farming methods lead to the creation of the Dust Bowl across the US states of Kansas, Oklahoma, Texas, Colorado, and New Mexico. Famine forces 300,000 people to abandon their farms.

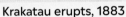
Krakatau erupts, 1883

1931 After heavy rain, the Yangtze River in China rises to 95 ft (29 m) above its normal level, flooding large areas of the country and destroying crops. In the floods and famine that follow, about 3.7 million people die.

1935 American Charles Richter invents the Richter scale to measure earthquake magnitude (size).

1946 The United Nations International Children's Emergency Fund (UNICEF) is founded to provide emergency aid to children in war or a natural disaster.

1953 A storm surge in the North Sea hits the Netherlands with 13-ft (4-m) waves, killing 1,800 people. It also produces 8-ft (2.5-m) waves in Essex, England, killing 300 people.

1958 Lituya Bay, Alaska, is hit by the largest local tsunami

in recent history, when a massive landslide produces a wave 1,725 ft (525 m) high.

1960 In May, the largest earthquake ever recorded, measuring 9.5, hits Chile, causing tsunamis that affect Chile, Peru, Hawaii, and Japan.

1968-1974 A seven-year drought occurs in the Sahel region of Africa. By 1974, 50 million people are relying on food from international aid agencies.

1970 An earthquake measuring 7.7 occurs off the coast of Peru, causing a massive avalanche and mudslide on the Nevados Huascarán Mountain, which kills 18,000 people.

1971 The worst hurricane (tropical cyclone) in history hits Bangladesh with winds up to 155 mph (250 kph) and a 25-ft (7.5-m) storm surge. The estimated death toll ranges from 300,000 to one million people.

1976 On July 28, an earthquake measuring 7.8 hits Tangshan, China, where 93 percent of the city's mud-brick houses collapse. The earthquake crushes 242,000 people to death.

1979 After a worldwide vaccination campaign, the WHO announces that it has successfully eradicated smallpox.

1984-1985 An extended drought in Ethiopia and Sudan in eastern Africa kills 450,000 people.

1985 On November 13, the eruption of Nevado del Ruiz in Colombia causes a mudslide that covers the town of Armero with 130 ft (40 m) of mud, killing 22,800 people.

1985 An earthquake measuring 8.1 hits Mexico City, killing more than 8,000 people and leaving 30,000 homeless.

1988 In Armenia, an earthquake measuring 6.9 causes newly built apartment buildings to collapse, killing 25,000 people.

1991 Mount Pinatubo in the Philippines erupts in June, ejecting so much debris into the atmosphere that global temperatures drop for 15 months.

Floods, England, 1953

Tornado in US Midwest

1992 In August, Hurricane Andrew strikes the Bahamas and Florida and Louisiana in the US, killing 65 people and causing $20 billion worth of damage.

1992 In December, a 85-ft- (26-m-) high tsunami hits Flores, Indonesia, killing 2,000, and making 90,000 homeless.

1993 Summer flooding on the Mississippi and Missouri Rivers in the US causes $12 billion worth of damage.

1995 In Kobe, Japan, 5,500 die as buildings collapse in a 7.2 earthquake.

1997 In September, wildfires in Indonesia destroy more than 741,000 acres (300,000 hectares) of forest, creating a widespread haze of pollution.

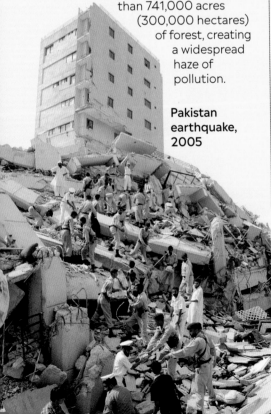

Pakistan earthquake, 2005

1998 Flooding in Bangladesh caused by a very strong El Niño kills 2,000 people and leaves 30 million homeless.

1998 In October, Hurricane Mitch strikes Central America, killing 11,000 and leaving 1.5 million homeless.

1999 On May 3, a tornado outbreak in Oklahoma sees 50 tornadoes rip across the state in one day, killing 40 people.

1999 An earthquake along Turkey's North Anatolian Fault destroys 150,000 buildings in Izmit, killing 17,000 people.

2001 In January, an earthquake in Gujarat, India, flattens 400,000 buildings, killing 20,000 people.

2002 Severe Acute Respiratory Syndrome (SARS), an unknown viral disease, appears in Guangdong, China.

2003 On December 27, an earthquake destroys the city of Bam, Iran, killing 26,000 people.

2004 On December 26, a tsunami in the Indian Ocean kills more than 230,000 people.

2005 On October 8, 86,000 die in a 7.6 earthquake in northern Pakistan and parts of Kashmir.

2008 Cyclone Nargis strikes Burma (Myanmar) on May 2. Catastrophic floods kill more than 138,000 people.

2008 On May 12, a magnitude 8.0 earthquake kills 68,000 people in Sichuan, China.

2009 The Black Saturday bushfires of February 7 sweep through southeast Australia.

2010 Up to 100,000 die in Haiti when an earthquake strikes the most populated part of the country on January 12.

2010 On August 8, heavy rain triggers a mudslide that kills more than 1,470 people in Gansu province, China.

2011 Christchurch, New Zealand, is struck by quakes in February and June.

2012 Extreme weather plagues the US: a severe heatwave and drought, month-long wildfires in the American West, and Hurricane Sandy, which claims 196 lives.

2013 In November, super-typhoon Haiyan (Yolanda)—the most powerful storm to ever hit land—kills 6,000 people and makes 4 million homeless in the Philippines.

2014 More than 7,000 people are killed across western Africa following an Ebola virus outbreak in March.

2015 An earthquake measuring 7.8 shakes the city of Kathmandu, Nepal, killing nearly 9,000 and injuring 22,000.

2016 Around 25 percent of Zimbabwe's population face food shortages after the country was hit by severe drought.

Health workers, SARS outbreak, 2002

2017 Floods in India, Nepal, and Bangladesh affect the lives of about 40 million people and kill more than 2,000.

2018 More than 4,000 people die and around 70,000 are evacuated after an earthquake and tsunami hit the island of Sulawesi in Indonesia.

2019-2020 Bushfires in Australia claim the lives of 33 people and burn around 42 million acres (17 million hectares) of land.

2020 A flu-like virus, called coronavirus (COVID-19) that started spreading in 2019 is declared a pandemic in March.

2021 La Cumbre Vieja, on the island of La Palma, Spain, continuously erupts for about 85 days, destroying acres of land and thousands of buildings.

2022 A massive eruption of the Hunga Tonga-Hunga Ha-apai volcano in the Pacific Ocean covered nearby islands in ash, triggered tsunamis, and sent shock waves around the world.

Find out **more**

You can find out more about natural disasters by visiting places mentioned in this book. You could investigate London's Thames Barrier, visit volcanic geysers in Yellowstone National Park, or take a trip back in time to Pompeii, Italy. There is lots of information on the Internet, too.

PLACES TO VISIT

Many large cities have museums that feature in-depth exhibits about Earth's weather, structure, and space. Visit the library or search the Internet to find out about natural history museums in your area.

Smithsonian Institution
Washington, D.C.
www.si.edu

American Museum of Natural History
New York, New York
www.amnh.org

Field Museum
Chicago, IL
www.fieldmuseum.org

California Academy of Sciences
San Francisco, CA
www.calacademy.org

Yellowstone

The world's first national park owes its creation to its spectacular geological features. Its geysers, hot springs, and bubbling mud are signs of an underground magma chamber.

Yellowstone National Park, founded in 1872

RICHTER SCALE

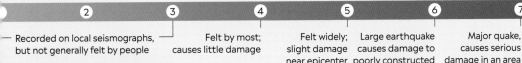

The intensity of an earthquake is measured using the Richter scale.

2	3	4	5	6	7	8	9
Recorded on local seismographs, but not generally felt by people	Felt by most; causes little damage	Felt widely; slight damage near epicenter	Large earthquake causes damage to poorly constructed buildings within tens of miles	Major quake, causes serious damage in an area up to 60 miles (100 km) across	Great quake causing destruction and death for 60 miles (100 km)	Rare great quake causing major damage across 600 miles (1,000 km) or more

USEFUL WEBSITES

- **www.tsunami.gov** follows tsunamis worldwide
- **www.tsunami.org** for the Pacific Tsunami Museum
- **noaa.gov/weather** for the US National Weather Service
- **www.panda.org** for the Worldwide Fund for Nature's information on climate change
- **www.weather.com** for global weather forecasts
- **www.epa.gov/climate-change** for global warming info
- **www.who.int** for information on health risks from the World Health Organization

Radar truck used by storm trackers

Category	1	2	3	4	5
Description	Weak	Moderate	Strong	Very strong	Devastating
Wind mph (kph)	75–95 (120–153)	96–110 (154–177)	111–130 (178–209)	131–155 (210–249)	156+ (250+)
Storm surge ft (m)	4–5 (1.2–1.5)	6–8 (1.6–2.4)	9–12 (2.5–3.7)	13–18 (3.8–5.5)	18+ (5.5+)
Damage	Minimal: some tree damage	Moderate: major damage to mobile homes and roofs	Extensive: mobile homes destroyed; trees blown down	Extreme: small buildings lose roofs; windows blown in	Catastrophic: roofs of many large buildings lost; storm surges

Hurricane scale

The Saffir-Simpson Scale classifies hurricanes by the strength of sustained wind speeds. Short gusts may reach faster speeds. Less than one percent of hurricanes are category 5.

Glossary

ACID RAIN Rain made more acidic by air pollution from vehicle exhausts and emissions from factories.

AFTERSHOCK A smaller earth tremor after the main shock of an earthquake. Aftershocks may continue for months.

AIR MASS A body of air with a uniform temperature over thousands of miles within the troposphere.

ATMOSPHERE The layer of gases that surrounds Earth.

AVALANCHE A large mass of snow sliding down a mountainside.

BACTERIA (singular bacterium) Microscopic single-celled organisms that lack a nucleus. Some can cause disease.

BORE A giant wave from an abnormally high tide that rushes up low-lying rivers.

BUOY A float anchored in water, usually to mark a position. Ocean-monitoring devices can be attached to buoys.

CARBON A nonmetallic element that occurs in the form of graphite, diamond, and charcoal, and in many compounds.

CLIMATE The regular pattern of weather.

CRATER A bowl-shaped depression at the mouth of a volcano or caused by the impact of a meteorite.

CRUST Earth's thin, rocky outer layer.

CUMULONIMBUS CLOUD A towering white or gray cloud that may bring thunderstorms or hail.

Crater of Mount Vesuvius in Italy

DROUGHT A long period with little or no rainfall.

DUST DEVIL A small, twisting wind that lifts dust and debris into the air.

EARTHQUAKE A series of vibrations in Earth's crust, caused by movement at a fault in or between tectonic plates.

EL NIÑO A weather pattern that causes warm water currents in the Pacific Ocean to flow east instead of west. It occurs every few years and can disrupt the weather around the world.

EMBANKMENT A bank of earth or stone, often used to protect an area from floods.

ENVIRONMENT The conditions and surroundings in which something exists.

EPICENTER The point on Earth's surface directly above the focus of an earthquake.

EPIDEMIC An outbreak of a contagious disease that spreads rapidly.

ERUPTION An outpouring of hot gases, lava, and other material from a volcano.

EVACUATION An organized departure of residents from an area.

FAULT A fracture in Earth's crust along which rocks have moved. Transform faults occur in areas where tectonic plates slide past one another.

FLASH FLOOD A flood that occurs suddenly after heavy rain.

FLOOD An overflow of water onto ground that is usually dry.

FLOOD DEFENSES Structures that redirect floodwater to avoid flooding.

FLOOD PLAIN An area of flat land on a river where the river naturally floods.

FOCUS A point within Earth's crust where an earthquake originates.

FOSSIL FUEL A fuel such as coal or oil that is derived from the organic remains buried beneath the ground.

FRONT The forward-moving edge of an air mass. A cold front is the leading edge of a cold air mass; a warm front is the leading edge of a warm air mass.

Aialik Glacier in Alaska

GLACIER A mass of year-round ice and snow that is capable of flowing slowly downhill. The largest glaciers are the Antarctic and Greenland ice sheets.

GLOBAL WARMING A gradual increase in average temperature worldwide.

GROUNDWATER Water that pools in, or flows through, rocks beneath the surface.

HABITAT An organism's natural home.

HAILSTONE A hard pellet of ice that falls from a cumulonimbus thundercloud.

HOT SPOT A site of volcanic activity far from the edges of the tectonic plates caused by magma rising from the mantle.

HURRICANE A violent storm of twisting winds and torrential rain. They are known as cyclones in the Indian Ocean and typhoons in the Pacific Ocean.

ICE AGE A period of time when ice sheets cover a large part of Earth.

IRRIGATION A system of channels for supplying farmland with water.

LANDSLIDE A large mass of rock or soil that slides down a hillside or breaks away from a cliff.

LAVA Molten rock that erupts from a volcano. When underground, it is magma.

LEVEE A natural or artificial embankment that prevents a river from overflowing.

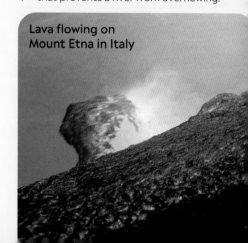
Lava flowing on Mount Etna in Italy

Rickshaw drivers ride through monsoon floods in Guwahati, India

LIGHTNING The visible flash during a thunderstorm when electricity is discharged from a cloud.

MAGMA Molten rock beneath Earth's surface. Above the ground, it is lava.

METEORITE A piece of solid material that has traveled from space, through Earth's atmosphere to land on Earth.

METEOROLOGIST A scientist who studies the weather.

MOLTEN Melted to form a hot liquid.

MONSOON A seasonal wind that, when it flows from the southwest, brings heavy summer rains to southern Asia.

OZONE LAYER The layer of gas in the stratosphere that helps protect Earth from the sun's harmful radiation.

PANDEMIC A disease outbreak that spreads to a vast number of people over a wide area.

PYROCLASTIC FLOW A fast-flowing and destructive outpouring of hot ash, rock, and gases from a volcano.

RADAR A system for detecting distant objects with reflected radio waves to determine size, position, and movement.

RICHTER SCALE A scale used for measuring the intensity of earthquakes.

SAFFIR-SIMPSON SCALE A scale used to measure the intensity of hurricanes.

SATELLITE An object that orbits a planet. Artificial satellites orbit Earth and monitor the weather, ground movements, and changes in sea level.

SEISMIC Caused by an earthquake.

SEISMOGRAM A record of seismic activity on paper or on a computer produced by a seismograph.

SEISMOGRAPH A device for detecting, recording, and measuring earth tremors.

SLUICE A human-made channel with a gate for regulating water flow, used to redirect excess water in order to prevent flooding.

SMOG Fog polluted with smoke.

SONAR A system that detects underwater surfaces with reflected sound waves.

STORM SURGE An unusually high tide produced by the eye of a hurricane.

STRATOSPHERE The atmosphere layer above the troposphere, where the ozone layer is found.

SUNSPOT A dark area on the surface of the sun; magnetic forces hold back light.

SUPERCELL CLOUD A huge storm cloud that may produce a tornado.

TECTONIC PLATE One of about 20 pieces that make up Earth's crust. The parts that carry the continents are denser and thicker than the ocean parts.

THUNDER The sound of air expanding rapidly when it is heated by lightning.

TORNADO A spinning wind that appears as a funnel-shaped cloud reaching down to the ground.

TREMOR A shaking or vibrating movement.

TRIBUTARY A river or stream that flows into a larger one.

TROPOSPHERE The layer of the atmosphere closest to Earth's surface where all weather happens.

TSUNAMI Fast-moving ocean waves, generated by tectonic movements or by an object impacting the water's surface.

VENT An opening in a volcano through which lava or volcanic gases flow.

VIRUS An infectious microscopic package of chemicals in a protein coat. They invade and destroy living cells.

Coronavirus particles

VOLCANO An opening in Earth's crust through which lava escapes.

VOLCANOLOGIST A scientist who studies volcanoes.

VORTEX A spiraling mass of liquid or gas. A tornado's center is a vortex.

WATERSPOUT A tornado over water; a spinning column of mist and spray.

WAVE CREST A wave's highest point.

WAVE TROUGH A wave's lowest point.

Supercell cloud

Index

ABC

acid rain 57
Africa 49, 57
  see also individual countries
aid 22, 49
AIDS 58, 61
air pressure 33, 36, 37, 38, 42
airplanes, 35, 38, 39
Alaska 16, 17, 32
ancient Greece 10
Antarctica 55
Arctic 54
argon 32
Asia
  desertification 57
  earthquakes and tsunamis 18, 20–25
  wildfires 50, 51
asteroids 14, 63
Aswan High Dam 44
Atlantic Ocean 8, 36
atmosphere 32–33, 55
Australia 47, 50, 52
avalanches 30–31
bacteria 58, 60
Banda Aceh 19
Bangladesh, floods 46, 47
bird flu 62
blast fishing 57
boats 19, 23, 46
Britain 39, 45
bubonic plague 58, 60
buoys 24
Burma (Myanmar) 38
bushfires 50
California 7, 10, 11, 31, 50–51, 53
Canada 33
Canary Islands 62, 63
carbon dioxide 55
carbon monoxide 56
Caribbean Islands 11, 38
cars, pollution 56
CFCs 56
Chile 56
China 17, 46, 62
cholera 22, 59, 61
cinder cone volcano 26
climate 32
climate change 54–57
clouds 32, 34, 36
coastal erosion 31
common cold 58
coral reefs 54, 57
coronavirus (COVID-19) 60–61
COVAX 61
crops 48, 58
cyclones 36, 38, 39

DEF

dams 44, 46, 47
deforestation 56
deserts 33, 43, 48, 57
diseases 7, 22, 51, 58–61, 62
dogs, rescue 13, 30
Doppler radar 45
drought 7, 48–49, 52
dust devils 43
dust storms 33
Earth 6, 8
earthquakes 6, 8, 10–13
  measurement 18, 69
  and tsunamis 14–25
Egypt 44
Eiffel Tower, Paris 34
El Niño 37, 47
El Salvador 31
electricity 34
elephants 22
epidemic 60
Equator 33
Ethiopia 49
Europe 45, 50
  see also individual countries
evacuation 22, 28, 40, 41, 47
evaporation 34
extinctions 63
famine 49
farming 28, 48, 49, 50, 54
Finding Individuals for Disaster Response (FINDER) 13
firefighters 12, 50, 52, 53
fish and fishing 23, 48, 57
fleas 58
floodgates 24
floods 41, 44–47
flu 60, 62
forests and forest fires 7, 50, 51, 56
fossil fuels 54, 56, 57
France, Paris 34
fulgurite 35
fungi 58, 59

GHIJL

gases, climate change 56, 57
geologists 55
Germany 45
glaciers 45
gravity 32
Great Plains 42, 49
Greenland 54, 55
groundwater 48–49
hailstones 35
Haiti, earthquake 11
Hawaii 6, 9, 26, 27, 63
health education 60, 61
heat and heatwaves 8, 51
helicopters 30, 46, 52–53
HIV/AIDS 58, 61
Hong Kong 62
hurricane hunters 35, 38, 39
hurricanes 35, 36–41, 69
ice 35, 45
  polar 54, 55
ice storms 33
Iceland, volcanoes 27, 28
India 14, 18, 19, 44, 48, 60
Indian Ocean 18–19, 24, 36
Indonesia 15, 18–19, 29, 52
industry, and climate change 56
Ireland 59
isobars 33
Italy, volcanoes 29, 62
Japan
  earthquakes and tsunamis 6, 12–13, 20–21, 23–25
  volcanoes 27
landslides 14, 17, 30, 31, 63
lava 27, 29
Leeuwenhoek, Anton van 58
levees 41
lichens 28
lightning 34, 35, 50
Lisbon, Portugal 6
London, flood barrier 45

MNOP

magma 9, 26, 27, 28
malaria 7, 58, 60, 61
Mayans 46
mega-tsunami 62–63
memorials 25
meteorites 14
Mexico, mega-tsunami 63
microorganisms 58, 61
microscopes 58
Miki Endo 25
Mississippi River 47
monsoon 44, 52
mosquitoes 61
mosses 28
Mount Vesuvius 29, 62
mountain ranges 9
MRSA 61
Naples, Italy 62
NASA 13, 63
Near Earth Object (NEO) 62, 63
Nepal 12
Netherlands 46
New Orleans, hurricane 40–41
Nile River 44
nitrogen 32
Noah's ark 46
North America. *see* USA
nuclear power plant
  Fukushima 21, 22, 23
oceanographers 24, 25
oceans 9, 54
  see also tsunamis; individual oceans
oxygen 32, 56
ozone 56
Pacific Ocean 24, 36, 37
pandemics 60–61
Pangaea 8
Philippines, volcanoes 7, 29, 32
plague 58, 60
polar bears 54
pollution 56, 57
Pompeii 29, 62
population growth 7
Poseidon 10
potato blight 59
pyroclastic flow 29

RST

radar 45
radiation 21, 23
rainfall
  acid 57
  average global 45
  floods 46, 47
  torrential 34, 44
rainforest, fires 51
rats 60
refugee camps 22, 49
rescue workers 13, 21, 23, 30, 41, 45
Richter, Charles, and Richter scale 10, 69
rockfalls 31
San Andreas fault line 9, 10
sand dunes 48
satellites 7, 25, 34, 38
sea level rises 55
seasons 54
seismic waves 10
seismogram 18
seismographs 11, 18, 24
seismoscope 11, 18
shield cone volcano 26
smallpox 58, 59
smog 52, 56
snow *see* avalanches
soil 51, 57
Somalia 18
sonar maps 25
South America 9, 37, 50
Southeast Asia 50, 51
Sri Lanka 18, 19
storm chasers 42
storm clouds 32, 33, 35
storm surge 37, 38, 40, 41
stratovolcano 26
Sumatra, Indonesia 15, 18–19
sun 6, 32, 55, 56
tectonic plates 8–9
telescopes 63
Thailand, tsunami 22
Thames Barrier, London 45
thunderstorms 32, 34–35
tidal bores 17
Tohoku earthquake 17
tornadoes 42–43
torrential rain 34, 44
tropical storms 36–37
troposphere 32
tsunamis 6, 14–25, 63
twisters 42
typhoons 36

UVWY

USA
  coastal erosion 31
  drought and famine 49
  earthquakes 10, 11
  floods 47
  hurricanes 37, 39, 40–41
  ice storms 33
  tornadoes 42
  volcanoes 28, 62
  wildfires 50–51, 53
  see also Alaska; Hawaii
vaccination 60, 61
Virgin Islands 16
viruses 58, 60
volcanoes 6, 7, 26–29
  future risks 62
  tectonic plates 8, 9
    and tsunamis 14
volcanologists 27, 28
warning systems, tsunami 24–25
water
  clean, access to 59, 60
  evaporation 34
  groundwater 48–49
  humidity 32
  temperature 32
waterspouts 43
waves 44
  see also tsunamis
weather forecasts and instruments 7, 42, 45
wildfires 7, 50–53
winds, 33, 37, 39, 42, 43
  see also hurricanes
Yangtze River 46
Yellowstone National Park 62

Acknowledgments

The publisher would like to thank the following people for their help with making the book: Ashwin Khurana for text editing, Vijay Kandwal for color work, Priyanka Sharma-Saddi for the jacket, and Joanne Penning for proofreading and the index.

The publisher would like to thank the following for their kind permission to reproduce their photographs:
(Key: a-above; b-below/bottom; c-center; f-far; l-left; r-right; t-top)
© Michael Holford: (26ca). **Alamy Stock Photo:** ES Travel 12clb; Leopold von Ungern 12cl; Yuriko Nakao / Reuters 18-19tc; Reuters 18cl; Reuters / Chaiwat Subprasom 22-23b; FLPA 27tl; NatPar Collection 28clb; Aerial Archives 31cr; Andrew Parker 32br; Xinhua 39br; ZUMA Press, Inc. 42bc/EW Box; Frank Schultze 44-45cl; PhotoBliss 48cl; Arthur Rothstein / JT Vintage / Glasshouse Images 49tl; Jane Barlow / PA Images 55clb; Norbert Wu / Minden Pictures 57cr; Smith Collection / Gado Images 58-59bc; Reuters 61bc; Ed Darack / RGB Ventures / SuperStock 63cra. **Associate Professor Ted Bryant, Associate Dean of Science, University of Wollongong** (13 t). **Corbis:** Jim Reed 2br; Dan Lamont 3br; Alfio Scigliano/Sygma 5; Frans Lanting 7tr; 9c; Academy of Natural Sciences of Philadelphia 10cr; Reuters 10bc; David de la Paz 11t; Kevin Schafer 9cr; Thomas Thompson/WFP/Handout/Reuters 16tl; Bazuki Muhammas/ Reuters 17bl; Yuriko Nakao 17tr; Dadang Tri/Reuters (14tl); Chaiwat Subprasom/Reuters 18-19b; Kyodo / Xinhua Press 21br; Chaiwat Subprasom/Reuters 21r; Reuters 22br; Owen Franken 23t; Kurt Stier 24cl; Patrick Robert/Sygma 24tr; Ryan Pyle 24bl; Andrea Comas/ Reuters 25br; Michael S. Yamashita 25cla; Jose Fuste Raga 27tr; Gary Braasch 28tl; Alfio Scigliano/Sygma 28-29bc; Alberto Garcia 29t; John Van Hasselt 30c; Lowell Georgia 30cr; S.P. Gillette 30l; Jonathan Blair 31cl; Reuters 31bl, 31bc; Christopher Morris 33bl; Frances Litman / All Canada Photos 36tr; epa 39tr; Irwin Thompson/Dallas Morning News 40bl; Smiley N. Pool/Dallas Morning News 40cr; Ken Cedeno 40tl; Vincent Laforet/Pool/Reuters 41tl; Irwin Thompson/Dallas Morning News 41br; 42c; Reuters 44bc; Jim Reed 45bc, 69 bl; Tom Bean 45cr; Reuters 46-47b; Brooks Kraft 47tr; Rafiqur Rahman/ Reuters 47tl; Romeo Ranoco/Reuters 47bc; Magnum: Philip Jones-Griffiths 47cr; Howard Davies 49br; Stephenie Maze 50c; Douglas Faulkner 51tl; Ed Kashi 51tr; Steven K. Doi/ZUMA 52-53; Dan Lamont 53b; Hans Strand 54–55; Erik de Castro/Reuters 61tr; Pallava Bagla 61t; Andy Crump, TDR, NIBSC 61br; Claro Cortes IV/Reuters 62br; Reuters 64br; Sally A. Morgan, Ecoscene (64bl); Ted Soqui (64tr) Gianni Dagli Orti (66bc); Reuters (65l); Vinve Streano (65br); Faisal Mahmood/Reuters 68bl; Reuters 68cr; Bettmann (67crb); Reuters 71t. **DK Images:** Courtesy of Glasgow Museum 2cr; Science Museum, London 23cr; Courtesy of the Museo Archeologico Nazionale di Napoli 29br; Michael Zabe CONACULTA-INAH-MEX. Authorized reproduction by the Instituto Nacional de Antropologia 46tr. *Dreamstime.com:* Luis Leamus (9tr). **Empics Ltd:** AP 14br; 15cr; Karim Khamzin/AP 15b; Wang Xiaochuan/AP 19tr; Roy Garner 19c; Lucy Pemoni/AP 21cr; Itsuo Inouye/AP Photo 29cr; Jordan Peter/PA 58bl; David Guttenfelder/AP 59tr; John Moore/AP 60bl. **FLPA - Images of Nature:** S. Jonasson 27 bl; Mario Laporta / Reuters 27br; Jim Reed 35 fbr; Peter Menzel 35c; 39tr; Ben Van den Brink/Foto Natura 50bl; Norbert Wu/Minden Pictures 57cr. **Getty Images:** Jimin Lai/AFP 2br; Getty Images / iStock: Tomislz 3cb; Getty Images / iStock: Luoman 4tl; Noburu Hashimoto 6b; Jim Sugar/Science Faction 6cr; Andres Hernandez / Hulton Archive 7br; Aaron McCoy/ Lonely Planet Images 7cl; Andres Hernandez/Getty Images News 7b; Getty Images / iStock: Tomislz 11br; Ronaldo Schemidt / AFP 13br; Jimin Lai/AFP 16cl; Getty Images: Archive Farms / Hulton Archive 14cr; Getty Images: DigitalGlobe 15tr; Sadatsugu Tomizawa / AFP 16-17bl; Getty Images: Jimin Lai / AFP 19bl; Yasuyoshi Chiba / AFP 20tl; NOAA: (20tr) DigitalGlobe 21tl; JIJI Press / AFP 20-21b; Yasuyoshil Chiba / AFP 20tl; DigitalGlobe 21tl; Yomiuri Shimbun / AFP 21cl; Getty Images News 20b, 21cl; The Asahi Shimbun 22tr; Kazuhiro Nogi / AFP 23t; Sankei 25tc; Jose Fuste Raga / Gamma-Rapho 27cra; Adek Berry 29clb; Vedros & Associates/The Image Bank 30cr; Getty Images / iStock: Twigymuleford 32crb; Handout / Getty Images News 33br; Joe Raedle 39tl; Ed Pritchard/Stone 39cl; Anadolu Agency 42 bc; Chandan Khanna 37c; AFP 44 tr; triloks 60br; Roger Ressmeyer / Corbis 62 tl; Scott Barbour / Stringer 47bc Scott Barbour 47c; 49 crb; Time Life Pictures 49tl; John Moore 49cr. Jason South / The Age / Fairfax Media 50-51 br. The AGE / Fairfax Media 50-51b; Jenny Evans 53tr; Getty Images / iStock: Luoman 56-57bl; Fraser Hall/Robert Harding World Imagery 66–67 bc. **NASA:** 52 bl; Goddard Space Flight Center Scientific Visualization Studio Thanks to Rob Gerston (GSFC) for providing the data. (54 clb); Goddard Space Flight Center Scientific Visualization Studio 54 crb; NASA 56tr; Don Davis 63br; Aubrey Gemignan 13tr. **Magnum:** Steve McCurry 48 bl; Jean Gaumy 57tl. **Science Photo Library:** NOAA 1, 36b, 40-41c, 45br; Planetary Visions Ltd 2c; NASA 4 tr; 6tr; 5 tr; Planetary Visions Ltd 5tl; Eye of Science 7cr; Stephen & Donna O'Meara 10cl; Digital Globe, Eurimage 11tl; 11t;. 14 clb; David Ducros 21tl; US Geological Survey 21b; Georg Gerster 22cl; NASA 23bl; Zephyr 23br; Bernhard Edmaier 26-27b; Mauro Fermariello 27cl; Mauro Fermariello 27crb; Mark Clarke 30br; NASA 32c; Jean-Loup Charmet 34tl; Kent Wood 34–35c; Jim Reed 35cb; Colin Cuthbert 36tr; Chris Sattlberger 38cl, 38cr; NOAA J.G. Golden 43 br;; Novosti Photo Library 48tr; NASA 50tr, 54cl, 54cr; Alexis Rosenfield 54tl; British Antarctic Survey 55cr; BSIG, M.I.G./ BAEZA 56cl; David Hay Jones: 56tl; Simon Fraser 57br; John Burbridge 58tr; Eye of Science 58c; Andrew Syred 59cl; Astrid & Hanns-Frieder Michler (59c); James King-Holmes 60tl; AJ Photo/ Hop Americain 61c; CDC/C. Goldsmith/J. Katz/S. Zaki; 62-63 bl; NASA 63tl, 63 br; 64–65; Russell Kightley 65c; Mehau Kulyk 66tl; Photo Researchers 66t; Bettmann 67bc; Eric Nguyen/Jim Reed Photography 68tl; Jeremy Bishop 70br; Dr Linda Stannard; UCT 71c Jim Reed 71bc. **Rex Features:** HXL 2tr; Masatoshi Okauchi 3cr; SIPA 14 b; RSR 17br; HXL 18 cl; IJO 19 br; Masatoshi Okauchi 20tr; Sipa Press 24-25b. **Photolibrary.com:** Warren Faidley/OSF 2tl; Warren Faidley/OSF 37b; Warren Faidley/OSF 37tr; NOAA 37 tl; Warren Faidley/OSF 42cl, 42c, 42cr. Warren Faidley/OSF 43t; Mary Beth Angelo 43br. Sarah Puttnam/Index Stock Imagery 49tr. Mary Plage/ OSF (67 cra). **Reuters:** Amateur Video Grab 15t; China Photos 46-4 bl; Amit Dave 48-49 bc Reuters 27br. Reuters: Claro Cortes (62br). **Kyodo News:** 21cra. **Rob Francis:** 9b. **Tony Friedkin/Sony Pictures Classics/ZUMA:** 12-13. **Nick Cornish (NCH):** 18t; **SS/Keystone USA (KUS):** 18cl **US Marine Corps:** Gunnery Sgt. Shannon Arledge (33b **U.S. Air Force:** Staff Sgt. Kristen Pittman / c / o 403rd Wing (35cr). **University of Wisconsin, Madison:** Cooperative - Institute for Meteorological Satellite Studies: 38crb. **Still Pictures:** W. Ming 57tr **Jeff Vanuga:** 62-63 t.**The Art Archive:** (66 bl). **www.bridgeman.co.uk:** The Great Wave of Kanagawa, from 'Thirty six views of Mount Fuji', c.1831, colour woodblock print (detail) by Hokusai, Katsushika, Tokyo Fuji Art Museum, Tokyo, Japan 3bl; The Great Wave of Kanagaw from 'Thirty six views of Mount Fuji', c.1831, colour woodblock print (detail) by Hokusai, Katsushika, Tokyo Fuji Art Museum, Tokyo, Japan 10tl. **Panos Pictures:** Tim A. Hetherington 15cl; Dieter Telemans 16tr Dean Chapman 20tl; Paul Lowe 52cr; Dean Sewell 53cl.

All other images © Dorling Kindersley.
For further information, see:
www.dkimages.com